GREAT TASTES

MEDITERRANEAN

First published in 2010 by Bay Books, an imprint of Murdoch Books Pty Limited
This edition published in 2010.

Murdoch Books Australia
Pier 8/9
23 Hickson Road
Millers Point NSW 2000
Phone: +61 (0) 2 8220 2000
Fax: +61 (0) 2 8220 2558
www.murdochbooks.com.au

Murdoch Books UK Limited
Erico House, 6th Floor
93–99 Upper Richmond Road
Putney, London SW15 2TG
Phone: +44 (0) 20 8785 5995
Fax: +44 (0) 20 8785 5985
www.murdochbooks.co.uk

Chief Executive: Juliet Rogers
Publishing Director: Kay Scarlett
Publisher: Lynn Lewis
Senior Designer: Heather Menzies
Designers: Transformer Creative
Production: Kita George
Index: Jo Rudd

ISBN: 9780681657915

PRINTED IN CHINA

OVEN GUIDE: You may find cooking times vary depending on the oven you are using. For fan-forced ovens, as a general rule, set the oven temperature to 20°C (35°F) lower than indicated in the recipe.

GREAT TASTES

MEDITERRANEAN

More than 120 easy recipes for every day

bay books

CONTENTS

MEDITERRANEAN CUISINE BASICS

The Mediterranean region is rich in resources and varied in landscape and stretches from Spain down to Morocco and Algeria, then follows the shores of the Mediterranean Sea to Tunisia, Libya, Egypt, Israel, Lebanon, Syria and Turkey in the east and Greece, Italy and southern France in the north.

There is no one Mediterranean cuisine. Because of the history of the region, it remains one of the most colourful and vibrant collections of cuisines in the world. However, you could almost define the Mediterranean landscape by the cultivation of olive trees and the use of olive oil. Other vital ingredients are vegetables such as zucchini (courgettes), tomatoes, eggplants (aubergines), capsicums (peppers) and garlic, as well as fruits, pulses and grains, pasta, fresh herbs, spices and nuts.

The reliance on seafood is a natural one while supplies of red meat can be more problematic due to the often inhospitable terrain further inland, which makes livestock farming difficult.

The Mediterranean diet has received a lot of attention over the past decade from dietitians and nutritionists. At present, there is much research into the theory that the incorporation of olive oil and abundant seafood and fresh fruit and vegetables into the diet, combined with minimal consumption of red meat and animal fats in the form of butter, cream and lard, may be associated with a low incidence of coronary heart disease, obesity, diabetes and cancer.

Many of the recipes in this book are derived from resourceful peasant cuisines with powerful basic ingredients such as garlic and anchovies, to enhance the flavour of fresh vegetables and simple cuts of meat.

A few tips for success

- Use top-quality ingredients, preferably when they are in season and at their peak. Tomatoes are a prime example so, wherever possible, use fresh tomatoes which have been ripened on the vine. Otherwise, use good-quality canned tomatoes such as Italian roma which are regarded as superior because they're processed at their peak condition.

- Use fresh herbs where possible. To store fresh herbs such as parsley, basil and coriander, rinse them briefly in cold water, then shake dry and wrap in damp paper towels.

- Ground spices differ in flavour if you toast and grind them yourself. Toast and grind a small amount and put them in an airtight container. If you have to rely on pre-ground spices, remember that they lose their flavour and aroma with age.

Essential ingredients

Anchovies A small fish from the herring family found mainly in southern European waters. Although anchovies can be eaten fresh, they are rarely found outside Mediterranean fishing ports as they are delicate and need to be eaten or processed quickly. More commonly, anchovies are cured and packed in oil, salt or brine and are readily available in cans or jars.

Arborio rice A short-grained plump rice imported from Italy. Used in both sweet and savoury dishes, arborio rice is particularly suitable for making risotto because the grains absorb a lot of liquid and become creamy but still retain their firmness.

Artichoke hearts The fleshy centres or 'heart' of the thistly artichoke head. They are available whole or quartered, canned or in jars, chargrilled or plain, in olive oil or brine.

Bocconcini Small mozzarella balls are known as bocconcini or baby mozzarella. A smooth, mild, unripened cheese originally made from buffalo milk but now usually made from cow's milk, bocconcini should be refrigerated covered in the whey in which it is sold. They will last for three weeks but should be discarded if they show signs of yellowing or taste sour.

Borlotti beans Slightly kidney-shaped, this large bean is a beautifully marked pale, pinkish brown with burgundy specks. Popular in Italy, borlotti beans have a nutty flavour and are used in soups, stews and salads.

Burghul Burghul is wheat which has been hulled, boiled or steamed, then dried and cracked. A staple in the Middle East, it requires little or no cooking. Sold coarsely or finely ground.

Arborio rice

Bocconcini (baby mozzarella)

Cannellini beans

Capers

Calasparra rice This white medium-grained Spanish rice is traditionally used to make paella. If it is not available, arborio, camaroli or vialone nano can be used instead.

Cannellini beans These white, kidney-shaped beans are also known as Italian haricot beans or white kidney beans. Mildly flavoured and slightly fluffy in texture when cooked, they are good all-purpose beans for use in soups, casseroles, stews and salads. Available fresh, dried or canned.

Capers The pickled buds of a shrub which grows wild in many parts of the Mediterranean. Capers have a sharp, sour taste and are sold in seasoned vinegar or packed in salt which needs to be rinsed off before use.

Cedro This is a citrus fruit, also known as citron, which looks like a large, rough lemon. It dates back to ancient times and is grown especially for the thick peel which is removed and candied. Cedro is available in some speciality shops.

Chickpeas One of the most versatile and popular legumes in many parts of the world, chickpeas were first grown in the Levant and ancient Egypt. Middle Eastern dishes, including hummus, have chickpeas as their basis. They can be boiled, roasted, ground, mashed and milled and are available dried or canned.

Chorizo A Spanish sausage, with many regional varieties, based on pork, paprika and garlic. Chorizo is sliced and served as tapas and is also cooked in paellas, stews and soups. It can be purchased in raw and smoked forms.

Couscous This cereal is processed from semolina and coated with wheat flour. Instant couscous cooks in about 5 minutes. Couscous is used in much the same way as rice is used in Asia — as a high-carbohydrate accompaniment to meat and vegetable dishes.

Feta cheese A soft, white cheese ripened in brine. Originally made from the milk of sheep or goats, but often now made with the more economical cow's milk. Feta cheese tastes sharp and salty and can be eaten as an appetizer, cooked or marinated, or incorporated in baked dishes.

Filo pastry Filo or phyllo is a paper-thin pastry made from flour and water. It is used widely in Eastern Mediterranean countries for the making of both sweet and savoury dishes.

Haloumi A salty Middle Eastern cheese made from ewe's milk. The curd is cooked, then matured in brine, often with herbs or spices. It is most often grilled or fried but can also be used in salads or on bread.

Kefalotyri cheese A very hard, scalded and cured sheep or goat's milk cheese with a mild flavour. Its use depends on its age. When young, it is a table cheese, at six months, it is used in cooking, and when more mature, it makes an excellent grating cheese. Parmesan or pecorino can be substituted.

Marsala A fortified wine from Marsala in Sicily that comes in varying degrees of dryness and sweetness. Dry Marsalas are used in savoury dishes and drunk as an aperitif. Sweet ones are suitable for putting in dessert dishes such as zabaglione and are also served with desserts.

Preserved lemons Used in many Moroccan dishes to give a distinctive lemony, salty flavour. To prepare for use in recipes, rinse preserved lemon and remove pulp with a spoon. Rinse rind and pat dry with paper towel, then cut as directed.

Puy lentils This tiny, dark green lentil is considered a delicacy in France and is relatively expensive. Unlike most other lentils, puy lentils keep their shape and have a firm texture after cooking. They are used mostly for making salads and side dishes.

Spanish sweet paprika Is also known as pimentón. It has a sweet, cool, smokey flavour.

Chickpeas

Chorizo

Lemons

Lentils

STARTERS

TZATZIKI

MAKES 2 CUPS

2 Lebanese cucumbers (about 300 g/11 oz)

400 g (14 oz) Greek-style natural yoghurt

4 garlic cloves, crushed

3 tablespoons finely chopped fresh mint

1 tablespoon lemon juice

chopped fresh mint, extra, to garnish

1 **Cut the cucumbers** in half lengthways, scoop out the seeds with a teaspoon and discard. Leave the skin on and coarsely grate the cucumber into a small colander. Sprinkle with a little salt and leave to stand over a large bowl for 15 minutes to drain off any bitter juices.

2 **Meanwhile,** stir together the yoghurt, garlic, mint and lemon juice in a bowl.

3 **Rinse the cucumber** under cold running water. Taking small handfuls, squeeze out any excess moisture. Combine the cucumber and yoghurt mixture and season, to taste. Refrigerate until ready to serve. Garnish with mint and serve as a dip with flatbread or as a sauce for seafood and meat.

TARAMASALATA

MAKES 1½ CUPS

5 slices white bread, crusts removed

80 ml (3 fl oz/⅓ cup) milk

100 g (4 oz) tin tarama (grey mullet roe) see Note

1 egg yolk

½ small onion, grated

1 garlic clove, crushed

2 tablespoons lemon juice

80 ml (3 fl oz/⅓ cup) olive oil

pinch of ground white pepper

1 Soak bread in the milk for 10 minutes. Press in a strainer to extract excess milk, then place in a food processor with the tarama, egg yolk, onion and garlic and process for 30 seconds, or until smooth. Mix in 1 tablespoon lemon juice.

2 With the motor running, slowly pour in the olive oil in a thin stream. Add the remaining lemon juice and white pepper. If the dip tastes too salty, add another piece of bread.

Note: Grey mullet roe is traditional, but smoked cod's roe also gives a lovely flavour.

̶ ̶M̶US

MAKES 3 CUPS

- 220 g (6½ oz/1 cup) dried chickpeas
- 2 tablespoons tahini
- 4 garlic cloves, crushed
- 2 teaspoons ground cumin
- 80 ml (3 fl oz./⅓ cup) lemon juice
- 3 tablespoons olive oil
- large pinch of cayenne pepper
- 1½ teaspoons
- extra lemon juice, optional
- extra virgin olive oil, to garnish
- paprika, to garnish
- chopped flat-leaf (Italian) parsley, to garnish

1 Put chickpeas in a bowl, add 1 litre (35 fl oz./4 cups) water, then soak overnight. Drain. Place in a large saucepan with 2 litres (70 fl oz/8 cups) water, or enough to cover the chickpeas by 5 cm (2 inches). Bring to the boil, then reduce the heat and simmer for 1 hour 15 minutes, or until the chickpeas are very tender. Skim any scum from the surface. Drain well, reserving the cooking liquid and leave until cool enough to handle. Pick through for any loose skins and discard them.

2 Combine the chickpeas, tahini, garlic, cumin, lemon juice, olive oil, cayenne pepper and salt in a food processor until thick and smooth. With the motor running, gradually add enough of the reserved cooking liquid, about 185 ml (6 fl oz/ ¾ cup), to form a smooth creamy purée. Season with salt or some extra lemon juice.

3 Spread onto flat bowls or plates, drizzle with the extra virgin olive oil, sprinkle with paprika and scatter parsley over the top. This is delicious served with warm pita bread or pide.

BEAN AND ROSEMARY DIP

MAKES 2 CUPS

2 x 310 g (11 oz) tins butter or cannellini beans

3 tablespoons olive oil

2 garlic cloves, crushed

1 tablespoon finely chopped rosemary leaves

250 ml (9 fl oz/1 cup) chicken or vegetable stock

2 teaspoons lemon juice

1 **Rinse and drain beans** and set aside. Heat olive oil in a saucepan and cook the garlic and rosemary for 1 minute, or until the garlic is softened. Add the beans and stock and bring to the boil. Reduce the heat and simmer for 3–4 minutes. Leave to cool.

2 **Blend or process** the mixture in batches until smooth. Add lemon juice and season, to taste. Serve with bread or grissini. This dip can be kept in the refrigerator in a covered container for several days.

ENADE

MAKES 1½ CUPS

400 g (14 oz) Kalamata olives, pitted

2 garlic cloves, crushed

2 anchovy fillets in oil, drained

2 tablespoons capers in brine, rinsed, squeezed dry

2 teaspoons chopped fresh thyme

2 teaspoons dijon mustard

1 tablespoon lemon juice

60 ml (2 fl oz/¼ cup) olive oil

1 tablespoon brandy, optional

1 Process all the ingredients in a food processor until they form a smooth consistency. Season with freshly ground black pepper. Spoon into a sterilized, warm jar (see Notes), seal and refrigerate for up to 2 weeks.

Notes: To sterilize storage jar, preheat the oven to 120°C (250°F/Gas ½). Wash the jar and lid in hot soapy water and rinse with hot water. Put the jar in the oven for 20 minutes, or until completely dry. Do not dry with a tea towel (dish towel).

If refrigerated, the oil in the tapenade may solidify, making it white. This will not affect the flavour of the dish. Bring the tapenade to room temperature before serving and the oil will return to a liquid state.

AÏOLI WITH CRUDITÉS

AÏOLI

4 garlic cloves, crushed

2 egg yolks

315 ml (10 fl oz/1¼ cups) light olive or vegetable oil

1 tablespoon lemon juice

pinch of ground white pepper

12 asparagus spears, trimmed

12 radishes, trimmed

½ telegraph (long) cucumber, deseeded, halved lengthways and cut into thick matchsticks

1 head of witlof (chicory/Belgian endive), leaves separated

1 **For the aïoli,** place garlic, egg yolks and a pinch of salt in a food processor and process for 10 seconds. With the motor running, add the oil in a thin, slow stream. The mixture will start to thicken. When this happens, add the oil a little faster. Process until all the oil is incorporated and the mayonnaise is thick and creamy. Stir in the lemon juice and pepper.

2 **Bring a saucepan of water** to the boil, add the asparagus and cook for 1 minute. Remove and plunge the spears into a bowl of iced water.

3 **Arrange the asparagus,** radish, cucumber and witlof decoratively on a platter and place the aïoli in a bowl on the platter. The aïoli can also be used as a sandwich spread or as a sauce for chicken or fish.

Notes: It is important that all the ingredients are at room temperature when making this recipe. Should the mayonnaise start to curdle, beat in 1–2 teaspoons boiling water. If this fails, put another egg yolk in a clean bowl and very slowly whisk it into the curdled mixture, one drop at a time, then continue with the recipe instructions. Many other vegetables, including green beans, baby carrots, broccoli and cauliflower florets, sliced capsicums (peppers) and cherry tomatoes are suitable for making crudités. Choose vegetables in season, when they are at their best.

BROAD BEAN DIP

SERVES 6

200 g (7 oz/ 1 cup) dried broad beans
  (fava or ful nabed—see Note)

2 garlic cloves, crushed

¼ teaspoon ground cumin

1½ tablespoons lemon juice

up to 75 ml (2½ fl oz) olive oil

2 tablespoons chopped flat-leaf (Italian)
  parsley, to garnish

flatbread, for serving

1 **Rinse the beans well,** then place in a large bowl and cover with 500 ml (17 fl oz/2 cups) of water and leave to soak overnight.

2 **If using peeled beans** (see Note), transfer them and their soaking water to a large heavy-based saucepan. If you are using the unpeeled brown beans, drain, then add them to the pan with 500 ml (16 fl oz/2 cups) fresh water. Bring to the boil, cover, and simmer over low heat for 5–6 hours. Check the water level from time to time and add a little boiling water, as necessary, to keep the beans moist. Do not stir, but shake the pan occasionally to prevent the beans sticking. Set aside to cool slightly. Most of the liquid will have evaporated.

3 **Purée the contents of the pan** in a food processor, then transfer to a bowl and stir in the garlic, cumin and lemon juice. Gradually stir in enough olive oil to give a dipping consistency, starting with about 50 ml (2 fl oz). As the mixture cools it may become thick, in which case you can stir through a little warm water to return the mixture to dipping consistency.

4 **Spread over a large dish** and sprinkle the parsley over the top. Serve with the flatbread, cut into triangles.

Note: The dried fava beans can be the ready-peeled white ones or the small, brown ones.

BABA GHANNOUSH

MAKES 1¾ CUPS

2 large eggplants (aubergines)

3 garlic cloves, crushed

½ teaspoon ground cumin

80 ml (3 fl oz/⅓ cup) lemon juice

2 tablespoons tahini

pinch of cayenne pepper

1½ tablespoons olive oil

1 tablespoon chopped flat-leaf (Italian) parsley

black olives, to garnish

1 Preheat oven to 200°C (400°F/Gas 6). Prick the eggplants several times with a fork, then cook over an open flame for about 5 minutes, until the skin is black and blistered. Transfer to a baking tin and bake for 40–45 minutes, or until eggplants are very soft and wrinkled. Place in a colander over a bowl to drain off any bitter juices. Leave for 30 minutes, or until cool.

2 Carefully peel the skin from the eggplants, chop the flesh and put it in a food processor with the garlic, cumin, lemon juice, tahini, cayenne pepper and olive oil. Process until smooth and creamy. Alternatively, use a potato masher or fork. Season with salt and stir in the parsley. Spread in a flat bowl or on a plate and garnish with the olives. Serve with flatbread or pide for dipping.

Note: If you prefer, omit the stage of cooking the eggplant over an open flame. Bake the eggplant in a baking tin in a (200°C/400°F/Gas 6) oven for 1 hour, or until very soft.

FRIED HALOUMI CHEESE

SERVES 6

400 g (14 oz) haloumi cheese

olive oil, for shallow-frying

2 tablespoons lemon juice

1 **Pat the haloumi dry** with paper towels and cut into 1 cm (½ inch) slices.

2 **Pour oil into a large frying pan** to 5 mm (¼ inch) depth and heat over medium heat.

3 **Add the cheese** and fry for 1 minute each side, or until golden. Remove pan from the heat and pour the lemon juice over the cheese. Season with freshly ground black pepper. Serve straight from the pan or on a serving plate, as part of a meze spread, with crusty bread to mop up the lemon and olive oil mixture.

MAKES 24

200 g (7 oz) packet vine leaves in brine

250 g (9 oz/1 cup) medium-grain rice

1 small onion, finely chopped

1 tablespoon olive oil

60 g (2 oz) pine nuts, toasted

2 tablespoons currants

2 tablespoons chopped dill

1 tablespoon finely chopped mint

1 tablespoon finely chopped flat-leaf
  (Italian) parsley

80 ml (3 fl oz/⅓ cup) olive oil, extra

2 tablespoons lemon juice

500 ml (17 fl oz/2 cups) chicken stock

1 Soak the vine leaves in cold water for 15 minutes, then remove and pat dry. Cut off any stems. Reserve some leaves to line the saucepan and discard any that have holes or look poor. Meanwhile, soak the rice in boiling water for 10 minutes to soften, then drain.

2 Place the rice, onion, olive oil, pine nuts, currants, herbs and salt and pepper, to taste, in a large bowl and mix well.

3 Lay some leaves vein-side-down on a flat surface. Place 1 tablespoon of filling in the centre of each one, fold the stalk end over the filling, then the left and right sides into the centre, and finally roll firmly towards the tip. The dolmades should resemble small cigars. Repeat with remaining filling and leaves.

4 Use reserved vine leaves to line the base of a large, heavy-based saucepan. Drizzle with 1 tablespoon olive oil, then add the dolmades, packing them tightly in one layer. pour the remaining oil and the lemon juice over them.

5 Pour the stock over the dolmades and cover with an inverted plate to stop the dolmades moving around while cooking. Bring to the boil, then reduce the heat and simmer, covered, for 45 minutes. Remove with a slotted spoon. Serve warm or cold. These can be served with lemon wedges.

Note: Unused vine leaves can be stored in brine in an airtight container in the fridge for up to a week.

TURKISH FILO PARCELS

MAKES 24

400 g (14 oz) feta cheese

2 eggs, lightly beaten

25 g (1 oz/¾ cup) chopped flat-leaf
(Italian) parsley

375 g (13 oz) filo pastry

80 ml (3 fl oz/⅓ cup) olive oil

1 Preheat the oven to 180°C (350°F/Gas 4). Lightly grease a baking tray. Crumble the feta into a large bowl using a fork or your fingers. Mix in the eggs and parsley and season with freshly ground black pepper.

2 Cover the filo pastry with a damp tea towel so it doesn't dry out. Remove one sheet at a time. Brushing each sheet lightly with olive oil, layer 4 sheets on top of one another. Cut the pastry into four 7 cm (2¾ inch) strips.

3 Place 2 rounded teaspoons of the feta mixture in one corner of each strip and fold diagonally, creating a triangle pillow. Place on the baking tray, seam-side-down, and brush with olive oil. Repeat with the remaining pastry and filling to make 24 parcels. Bake for 20 minutes, or until golden. Serve these as part of a large meze plate.

Note: Fillings for these filo parcels are versatile and can be adapted to include your favourite cheeses such as haloumi, gruyère, cheddar or mozzarella.

FRIED CIGAR PASTRIES

MAKES 12

500 g (1 lb 2 oz) English spinach
1 tablespoon olive oil
4 garlic cloves, crushed
200 g (7 oz) French shallots, finely chopped
75 g (3 oz/½ cup) crumbled feta cheese
1 egg, lightly beaten
3 tablespoons chopped flat-leaf (Italian) parsley
¼ teaspoon finely grated lemon zest
¼ teaspoon paprika
pinch of nutmeg
6 sheets filo pastry
125 g (5 oz) butter, melted
light olive oil, for deep-frying

1   Wash the spinach, leaving a substantial amount of water on the leaves. Place in a large saucepan, cover and briefly cook over low heat until just wilted. Tip the spinach into a colander and press out most of the excess liquid with a wooden spoon. When cool, squeeze dry.

2   Heat the olive oil in a frying pan, add the garlic and shallots and cook for 2 minutes, or until soft but not browned. Transfer to a bowl and add the crumbled feta cheese, egg, parsley, spinach and lemon zest. Season with the paprika, nutmeg and salt and pepper, and mix well..

3   Remove a sheet of filo and cover the rest with a damp tea towel to prevent them drying out. Brush the sheet with melted butter, then fold it in half lengthways. It should measure about 32 x 12 cm (13 x 5 inches). Cut it in half widthways. Brush with butter, place about 1 heaped tablespoon of filling at one end of each and spread it to within 1 cm (½ inch) of each side. Fold the sides over to cover the ends of the filling, continuing folds right up the length of the pastry. Brush with melted butter, then roll up tightly. Brush the outside with butter and seal well. Cover with a damp tea towel (dish towel) and prepare the rest.

4   Heat light olive oil in a deep frying pan to 180°C (350°F), or until a cube of bread browns in 15 seconds. Deep-fry the pastries in small batches until they turn golden. Serve warm or at room temperature.

ARANCINI

MAKES 12

500 g (1 lb 2oz/2¼ cups) short-grain white rice

¼ teaspoon saffron threads

2 eggs, beaten

100 g (4 oz/1 cup) freshly grated parmesan cheese

plain (all-purpose) flour, for coating

2 eggs, beaten, extra

100 g (4 oz/1 cup) dry breadcrumbs

oil, for deep-frying

FILLING

1 tablespoon olive oil

1 small onion, finely chopped

150 g (6 oz) minced (ground) pork and veal, or beef

170 ml (6 fl oz/⅔ cup) white wine

1 tablespoon tomato paste (concentrated purée)

2 teaspoons fresh thyme leaves

1 Bring 1 litre (35 fl oz/4 cups) water to the boil in a large saucepan and add the rice and saffron threads. Bring slowly back to the boil, then reduce the heat to a simmer. Cover and cook over low heat for 20 minutes, or until tender. Transfer to a large bowl and cool to room temperature. Stir in the egg and grated parmesan cheese.

2 For the filling, heat oil in a small frying pan over medium heat. Add the onion and cook for 2–3 minutes, or until soft. Add minced meat and cook for 2 minutes, or until it changes colour, pressing out any lumps. Add the wine and tomato paste. Reduce the heat and simmer for 3–4 minutes, or until the wine has evaporated. Stir in thyme and set aside to cool.

3 With wet hands, divide the rice mixture into 12 balls. Flatten each slightly, make an indent in the centre of each and place 2 heaped teaspoons of the filling into each ball. Close the rice around the filling.

4 Roll each ball in the flour, dip in the extra egg, then roll in the breadcrumbs. Refrigerate for 30 minutes.

5 Fill a deep heavy-based saucepan one third full of oil and heat to 180°C (350°F), or until a cube of bread dropped into the oil browns in 15 seconds. Deep-fry the balls in four batches for 2–3 minutes each, or until golden brown. Drain on crumpled paper towels. Serve warm or at room temperature.

BRUSCHETTA

MAKES 4

4 large slices of 'country-style' bread, such as ciabatta

1 garlic clove

drizzle of extra virgin olive oil

1 Grill (broil), chargrill or toast the bread until it is crisp. Cut the garlic clove in half and rub the cut edge over both sides of each bread slice. Drizzle a little olive oil over each bread slice. Use this delicious bread as base for toppings such as chopped tomatoes drizzled with olive oil and sprinkled with fresh basil leaves.

FRIED WHITEBAIT

SERVES 6

40 g (1½ oz/⅓ cup) plain (all-purpose) flour

30 g (1 oz/¼ cup) cornflour (cornstarch)

500 g (1 lb 2 oz) whitebait

2 teaspoons finely chopped flat-leaf (Italian) parsley

oil, for deep-frying

1 lemon, cut into wedges, for serving

1 Combine the sifted flours and parsley in a bowl and season well with salt and cracked black pepper. Fill a deep, heavy-based pan one-third full of oil and heat until a cube of bread dropped into the oil browns in 15 seconds. Toss a third of the whitebait in the flour mixture, shake off the excess flour, and deep-fry for 1½ minutes, or until pale and crisp. Drain well on crumpled paper towels. Repeat with the remaining whitebait, cooking in two batches.

2 Reheat the oil and fry the whitebait a second time in three batches for 1 minute each batch, or until lightly browned. Drain on paper towels and serve hot with lemon wedges.

STUFFED SARDINES

SERVES 4–6

1 kg (2 lb 4 oz) butterflied fresh sardines

60 ml (2 fl oz./¼ cup) olive oil

40 g (1½ oz/½ cup) soft white breadcrumbs

40 g (1¼ oz/¼ cup) sultanas

40 g (1¼ oz/¼ cup) pine nuts, toasted

20 g (1 oz) tin anchovies, drained, mashed

1 tablespoon finely chopped flat-leaf (Italian) parsley

2 spring onions (scallions), finely chopped

1 Preheat the oven to 200°C (400°F/Gas 6). Open out each sardine and place skin-side-up on a chopping board.

2 Heat half the oil in a frying pan, add the breadcrumbs and cook over medium heat, stirring until light golden. Drain on paper towels.

3 Put half the fried breadcrumbs in a bowl and stir in the sultanas, pine nuts, anchovies, parsley and spring onion. Season with salt and pepper. Spoon about 2 teaspoons of the mixture into each prepared sardine, then carefully fold up to enclose the stuffing.

4 Place the stuffed sardines in a single layer in a well-greased baking dish. Sprinkle any remaining stuffing over the top of the sardines, with the cooked breadcrumbs. Drizzle with the remaining olive oil and bake for 15–20 minutes.

HAM AND MUSHROOM CROQUETTES

MAKES 18

90 g (3 oz) butter

1 small onion, finely chopped

110 g (4 oz) cap mushrooms, finely chopped

90 g (3 oz/¾ cup) plain (all-purpose) flour

250 ml (4 fl oz/1 cup) milk

185 ml (6 fl oz/¾ cup) chicken stock

110 g (4 oz) ham, finely chopped

60 g (2 oz/½ cup) plain (all-purpose) flour, extra

2 eggs, lightly beaten

50 g (2 oz/½ cup) dry breadcrumbs

oil, for deep-frying

1 Melt the butter in a saucepan over low heat, add the onion and cook for 5 minutes, or until translucent. Add the mushrooms and cook over low heat, stirring occasionally, for 5 minutes. Add the flour and stir over medium-low heat for 1 minute, or until the mixture is dry and crumbly and begins to change colour. Remove from the heat and gradually add the milk, stirring until smooth. Stir in the stock and return to the heat, stirring until the mixture boils and thickens. Stir in the ham and some black pepper, then transfer to a bowl to cool for about 2 hours.

2 Roll 2 tablespoons of mixture at a time into croquette shapes 6 cm (2½ inches) long. Place the extra flour, beaten egg and breadcrumbs in three shallow bowls. Toss the croquettes in the flour, dip in the egg, allowing the excess to drain away, then roll in the breadcrumbs. Place on a baking tray and refrigerate for about 30 minutes.

3 Fill a deep, heavy-based saucepan one-third full of oil and heat to 180°C (350°F), or until a cube of bread dropped into the oil browns in 15 seconds. Deep-fry the croquettes, in batches, for 3 minutes, turning, until brown. Drain well.

Note: You can vary these croquettes very easily to suit your taste. For example, replace the ham with finely chopped chicken or flaked cooked fish and add your favourite finely chopped fresh herb.

EMPANADAS

MAKES ABOUT 15

2 eggs

40 g (1¼ oz) stuffed green olives, chopped

95 g (3 oz) ham, finely chopped

¼ cup (30 g/1 oz) grated cheddar cheese

3 sheets ready-rolled puff pastry, thawed

1 egg yolk, lightly beaten

1 **Place the eggs in a small saucepan,** cover with water and bring to the boil. Boil for 10 minutes, then drain and cool for 5 minutes in cold water. Peel and chop.

2 **Preheat the oven** to hot 220°C (425°F/Gas 7). Lightly grease two baking trays. Combine the egg, olives, ham and cheddar cheese in a large bowl.

3 **Cut about five 10 cm** (4 inch) rounds from each pastry sheet. Spoon a tablespoon of the filling into the centre of each round, fold the pastry over and crimp the edges to seal.

4 **Place the pastries on the trays,** about 2 cm (¾ inch) apart. Brush with egg yolk and bake in the centre or top half of the oven for 15 minutes, or until well browned and puffed. Swap the trays around after 10 minutes and cover loosely with foil if the empanadas start to brown too much. Serve hot.

BARBECUED PRAWNS WITH ROMESCO SAUCE

SERVES 6–8

30 raw large prawns (shrimp)

¼ teaspoon salt

ROMESCO SAUCE

4 garlic cloves, unpeeled

1 roma (plum) tomato, halved and seeded

2 long fresh red chillies

35 g (1 oz/¼ cup) blanched almonds

60 g (2 oz) sun-dried capsicums (peppers) in oil

1 tablespoon olive oil

1 tablespoon red wine vinegar

1 Peel the prawns, leaving the tails intact. Gently pull out the dark vein from each prawn back, starting at the head end. Mix with the salt and refrigerate for 30 minutes.

2 For the Romesco sauce, preheat the oven to 200°C (400°F/Gas 6). Wrap the garlic in foil, place on a baking tray with the tomato and chillies and bake for 12 minutes. Spread the almonds on the tray and bake for another 3–5 minutes. Leave to cool for 15 minutes.

3 Transfer almonds to a small blender or food processor and blend until finely ground. Squeeze the garlic and scrape the tomato flesh into the blender, discarding the skins. Split the chillies and remove the seeds. Scrape the flesh into the

blender, discarding the skins. Pat the peppers dry with paper towels, then chop them and add to the blender with the oil, vinegar, some salt and 2 tablespoons water. Blend until smooth, adding more water, if necessary, to form a soft dipping consistency. Preheat a grill or lightly oiled barbecue.

4 Brush the prawns with a little oil and cook for 3 minutes, or until curled up and changed colour. Serve with the sauce.

Note: The sauce is traditionally served with seafood. It can be made up to 5 days in advance and stored in the refrigerator.

STUFFED MUSSELS

MAKES 18

18 black mussels

2 teaspoons olive oil

2 spring onions (scallions), finely chopped

1 garlic clove, crushed

1 tablespoon tomato paste (concentrated purée)

2 teaspoons lemon juice

3 tablespoons chopped flat-leaf (Italian) parsley

35 g (1¼ oz/⅓ cup) dry breadcrumbs

2 eggs, beaten

oil, for deep-frying

WHITE SAUCE

40 g (1½ oz) butter

30 g (1 oz/¼ cup) plain (all-purpose) flour

80 ml (3 fl oz/⅓ cup) milk

1 **Scrub the mussels** and remove the hairy beards. Discard any open mussels or those that don't close when tapped on the bench. Bring 250 ml (4 fl oz/1 cup) water to the boil in a saucepan, add the mussels, cover and cook for 3–4 minutes, shaking the pan occasionally, until the mussels have just opened. Remove them as soon as they open or they will be tough. Strain the liquid into a jug until you have 80 ml (3 fl oz/⅓ cup). Discard any unopened mussels. Remove the other mussels from their shells and discard one half shell from each. Finely chop the mussel meat.

2 **Heat the oil in a pan,** add the spring onion and cook for 1 minute. Add the garlic and cook for 1 minute. Stir in mussels, tomato paste, lemon juice, 2 tablespoons of the parsley, salt and pepper, then set aside to cool.

3 **For the white sauce,** melt the butter in a saucepan over low heat. Stir in the flour and cook for 1 minute, or until pale and foaming. Remove from the heat and gradually whisk in reserved mussel liquid, milk and some pepper. Return to the heat, stirring, for 1 minute, or until sauce boils and thickens. Reduce heat; simmer for 2 minutes. Set aside to cool.

4 **Spoon the mussel mixture** into the shells. Top each with some of the sauce, making the mixture heaped.

5 **Combine the crumbs** and remaining parsley. Dip the mussels in the egg, then press in the crumbs to cover the top. Fill a deep, heavy-based saucepan one third full of oil and heat to 180°C (350°F), or until a cube of bread dropped in the oil browns in 15 seconds. Cook mussels in batches for 2 minutes each batch. Remove with slotted spoon. Drain well. Serve hot.

SALT COD FRITTERS

MAKES 35

500 g (1 lb 2 oz) salt cod

1 large potato (200 g/7 oz), unpeeled

2 tablespoons milk

3 tablespoons olive oil

1 small onion, finely chopped

2 garlic cloves, crushed

30 g (1 oz/¼ cup) self-raising flour

2 eggs, separated

1 tablespoon chopped flat-leaf (Italian) parsley

olive oil, extra, for deep-frying

1 **Soak the cod in cold water** for 24 hours, changing the water regularly to remove as much salt as possible. Cook the potato in a pan of boiling water for 20 minutes, or until soft. When cool, peel and mash with the milk and 2 tablespoons of the olive oil.

2 **Drain the cod,** cut into large pieces and place in a saucepan. Cover with water, bring to the boil over high heat, then reduce the heat to medium and cook for 10 minutes, or until soft and there is a froth on the surface. Drain. When cool enough to handle, remove the skin and any bones, then mash well with a fork until flaky.

3 **Heat the remaining oil** in a small frying pan and cook the onion over medium heat for 5 minutes, or until softened and starting to brown. Add the garlic and cook for 1 minute. Remove from the heat.

4 **Combine the potato,** cod, onion, flour, egg yolks and parsley in a bowl and season. Whisk the egg whites until stiff, then fold into the mixture. Fill a large heavy-based saucepan one third full of olive oil and heat to 190°C (375°F), or until a cube of bread dropped into the oil browns in 10 seconds. Drop heaped tablespoons of mixture into the oil and cook for 2 minutes, or until puffed and golden. Drain and serve.

GARLIC PRAWNS

SERVES 4

| 1.25 kg (2 lb 12 oz) raw prawns (shrimp) |
| 80 g (3 oz) butter, melted |
| 185 ml (6 fl oz/¾ cup) olive oil |
| 8 garlic cloves, crushed |
| 2 spring onions (scallions), thinly sliced |

1 Preheat the oven to 250°C (500°F/Gas 10). Peel the prawns, leaving the tails intact. Pull out the vein from each back, starting at the head end. Cut a slit down the back of each prawn.

2 Combine the butter and oil and divide among four 500 ml (16 fl oz) cast iron pots. Divide half the crushed garlic among the pots.

3 Place the pots on a baking tray and heat in the oven for 10 minutes, or until the mixture is bubbling. Remove and divide the prawns and remaining garlic among the pots. Return to the oven for 5 minutes, or until the prawns are cooked. Stir in the spring onion. Season, to taste. Serve with bread to mop up the juices.

Note: Garlic prawns can also be made in a cast iron frying pan in the oven or on the stovetop.

~~FEL~~

150 g (6 oz/1 cup) dried split broad
    beans (see Note)

220 g (8 oz/1 cup) dried chickpeas

1 onion, roughly chopped

6 garlic cloves, roughly chopped

2 teaspoons ground coriander

1 tablespoon ground cumin

15 g (½ oz/½ cup) chopped flat-leaf
    (Italian) parsley

¼ teaspoon chilli powder

½ teaspoon bicarbonate of soda (baking
    soda)

3 tablespoons chopped coriander
    (cilantro) leaves

light oil, for deep-frying

1 **Place the broad beans** in a large bowl, cover well with water and soak for 48 hours. Drain, then rinse several times in fresh water.

2 **Place the chickpeas in a large bowl,** cover well with water and soak for 12 hours.

3 **Drain the broad beans** and chickpeas well, then purée in a food processor with the onion and garlic until smooth.

4 **Add the ground coriander,** cumin, parsley, chilli powder, bicarbonate of soda and fresh coriander. Season, to taste, and mix until well combined. Transfer to a large bowl and set aside for 30 minutes.

5 **Shape tablespoons of mixture** into balls, flatten to 4 cm (1½ inch) rounds, place on a tray and refrigerate for 20 minutes.

6 **Fill a deep, heavy-based saucepan** one third full of oil and heat to 180°C (350°F), or until a cube of bread dropped in the oil browns in 15 seconds. Cook the felafel in batches for 1–2 minutes, or until golden. Drain on paper towels. Serve hot or cold with hummus, baba ghannouj and pitta bread.

Note: Split broad beans, which are already skinned, are available from specialist stores. If whole broad beans are used, they will need to be skinned after soaking. To do this, squeeze each broad bean to allow the skin to pop off, or pierce each skin with your fingernail, then peel it off.

LAMB FILO FINGERS

MAKES 12

1 tablespoon olive oil
350 g (12 oz) lean minced (ground) lamb
1 small onion, finely chopped
2 garlic cloves, crushed
1 tablespoon ground cumin
1 teaspoon ground ginger
1 teaspoon paprika
1 teaspoon ground cinnamon
pinch of saffron threads, soaked in a little warm water
1 teaspoon harissa
2 tablespoons chopped coriander (cilantro) leaves
2 tablespoons chopped flat-leaf (Italian) parsley
3 tablespoons pine nuts, toasted
1 egg
6 sheets filo pastry
60 g (2 oz) butter, melted
1 tablespoon sesame seeds

1 **Preheat the oven** to 180°C (350°F/Gas 4). Lightly grease a large baking tray.

2 **Heat the oil in a large frying pan**, add the lamb and cook for 5 minutes, breaking up any lumps with the back of a wooden spoon. Add onion and garlic and cook for 1 minute. Add the spices, harissa, chopped coriander and parsley and cook for 1 minute, stirring to combine. Transfer to a sieve and drain to remove the fat.

3 **Place mixture in a bowl** and allow to cool slightly. Mix in the pine nuts and egg.

4 **Place a sheet of filo on the bench** with the shortest side facing you. Cover the remaining sheets with a damp tea towel to prevent them from drying out. Cut the sheet of filo into four equal strips lengthways. Brush one of the strips with melted butter and place another on top. Do the same with the other

two pieces. Place 1 tablespoon of the lamb mixture on each at the short end of the filo and roll each up, tucking in the ends to hold the mixture in and form each into a cigar shape. Repeat this process until you have used up all the filo and meat mixture.

5 **Place the lamb fingers** on the baking tray. Brush with any remaining melted butter and sprinkle with sesame seeds. Bake for 15 minutes, or until lightly golden.

6 **For the yoghurt sauce,** stir all the ingredients together in a small bowl. Serve filo fingers warm with sauce on the side.

PRAWN FRITTERS

MAKES 24 FRITTERS

60 g (2 oz/½ cup) plain (all-purpose)
  flour, sifted

55 g (2 oz/½ cup) besan (chickpea
  flour), sifted

1 teaspoon sweet paprika (pimentón)

4 large eggs, lightly beaten

4 spring onions (scallions), finely
  chopped

1 large handful flat-leaf (Italian) parsley,
  finely chopped

500 g (1 lb 2 oz) peeled and finely
  chopped raw prawns (shrimp), about
  800 g (1 lb 12 oz) unpeeled

125 ml (4 fl oz/½ cup) olive oil

lemon wedges, to serve

1 Combine the flours in a bowl with the paprika and
make a well in the centre. Pour in the beaten egg and mix in
gradually, then stir in 60 ml (2 fl oz/¼ cup) water to make a
smooth batter.

2 Add the spring onion, parsley and prawns and season
well. Rest the batter for at least 30 minutes.

3 Heat oil in a deep-sided frying pan over low–medium
heat. Working in batches, spoon in ½ tablespoons of batter per
fritter and flatten into a thin pancake. Cook for 2–3 minutes
each side, or until golden and cooked through.

4 Remove from the pan and drain on paper towel. Repeat
with the remaining batter to make 24 fritters. Season well and
serve with lemon wedges.

PICKLED SQUID

SERVES 4

1 kg (2 lb 4 oz) small squid
1 teaspoon salt
4 bay leaves
4 sprigs of oregano
10 whole black peppercorns
2 teaspoons coriander seeds
1 small red chilli, halved and seeded
625 ml (22 fl oz/2½ cups) good-quality white wine vinegar
2–3 tablespoons olive oil, to top up the jar

1 **To prepare the squid,** grasp each squid body in one hand and the head and tentacles in the other and pull apart to separate them. Cut the tentacles from the head by cutting below the eyes. Discard the head. Push out the beak and discard. Pull the quill from inside the body and discard. Under cold running water, pull away the skin (the flaps can be used). Cut into 7 mm (3/8 inch) rings.

2 **Place 2 litres (70 fl oz/8 cups) water** and 1 bay leaf in a large saucepan. Bring to the boil and add the squid and salt. Reduce the heat and simmer for 5 minutes. Drain and dry well.

3 **Pack squid rings** into a clean, dry 500 ml (17 fl oz/2 cup) jar with a sealing lid (see Note). Add the oregano, peppercorns, coriander seeds, chilli and remaining bay leaves. Then cover completely with the vinegar then gently pour in enough olive oil to cover by 2 cm (3/4 inch). Seal and refrigerate for 1 week before opening. When you are ready to serve, remove from the marinade, place on a serving dish and garnish with lemon wedges and chopped parsley.

Note: Wash the storage jar and lid in hot soapy water, rinse them well in hot water and then dry in a the oven at 120°C (250°F/Gas ½) for 20 minutes. Do not dry then with a tea towel (dish towel).

POLENTA SQUARES WITH MUSHROOM RAGU

SERVES 4

500 ml (16 fl oz/2 cups) vegetable stock or water

150 g (6 oz/1 cup) polenta

20 g (1 oz) butter

75 g (3 oz/¾ cup) grated parmesan cheese

5 g (¼ oz) dried porcini mushrooms

200 g (7 oz) Swiss brown mushrooms

300 g (11 oz) field mushrooms

125 ml (4 fl oz/½ cup) olive oil

1 onion, finely chopped

3 cloves garlic, finely chopped

1 bay leaf

2 teaspoons finely chopped thyme

2 teaspoons finely chopped oregano

15 g (½ oz/½ cup) finely chopped flat-leaf (Italian) parsley

1 tablespoon balsamic vinegar

25 g (¾ oz/¼ cup) grated parmesan cheese, extra

1 **Grease a 20 cm (8 inch)** square shallow cake tin. Place the stock and a pinch of salt in a large saucepan and bring to the boil. Add polenta in a steady stream, stirring constantly. Reduce heat and simmer, stirring frequently, for 15–20 minutes. Remove from the heat and stir in the butter and parmesan cheese. Spread the mixture into the tin and refrigerate for 20 minutes.

2 **Soak the porcini mushrooms** in 125 ml (4 fl oz/½ cup) boiling water for 10 minutes, or until softened, then drain, reserving 80 ml (3 fl oz/⅓ cup) liquid.

3 **Wipe the other mushrooms** with a damp cloth. Thickly slice the Swiss brown mushrooms, and coarsely chop the field mushrooms. Heat 80 ml (3 fl oz/⅓ cup) oil in a large frying pan, add the mushrooms, including the porcini mushrooms, cook for 4–5 minutes, then remove from the pan. Heat the

remaining oil in the pan and cook the onion and garlic over medium heat for 2–3 minutes, or until transparent.

4 **Add the reserved soaking liquid,** bay leaf, thyme and oregano to the pan, season and cook for 2 minutes. Return the mushrooms to the pan, add the parsley and vinegar and cook over medium heat for 1 minute, or until nearly dry. Remove the bay leaf and check the seasoning.

5 **Sprinkle extra parmesan cheese** over the polenta and heat under a medium grill (broiler) for 10 minutes, or until lightly browned and the cheese has melted. Then cut into four 10 cm (4 inch) squares.

6 **Place a polenta square** in the centre of each serving plate and top with mushroom mixture. Season with black pepper.

SERVES 6

175 g (6 oz) minced (ground) pork

175 g (6 oz) minced (ground) veal

3 garlic cloves, crushed

35 g (1 oz/⅓ cup) dry breadcrumbs

1 teaspoon ground coriander

1 teaspoon ground nutmeg

1 teaspoon ground cumin

pinch of ground cinnamon

1 egg

2 tablespoons olive oil

SPICY TOMATO SAUCE

1 tablespoon olive oil

1 brown onion, chopped

2 garlic cloves, crushed

125 ml (4 fl oz/½ cup) dry white wine

400 g (14 oz) tin chopped tomatoes

1 tablespoon tomato paste
  (concentrated purée)

125 ml (4 fl oz/½ cup) chicken stock

½ teaspoon cayenne pepper

80 g (3 oz/½ cup) frozen peas

1 Combine the pork, veal, garlic, breadcrumbs, spices, egg and season with salt and pepper in a bowl. Mix by hand until the mixture is smooth and leaves the side of the bowl. Refrigerate, covered, for 30 minutes.

2 Roll tablespoons of mixture into balls. Heat 1 tablespoon of olive oil in a frying pan and toss half the meatballs over medium–high heat for 2–3 minutes, or until browned. Drain on paper towels. Add the remaining oil, if necessary, and brown the rest of the meatballs. Drain on paper towels.

3 To make the sauce, heat oil in a frying pan over medium heat and cook the onion, stirring occasionally, for 3 minutes, or until translucent. Add the garlic and cook for 1 minute. Increase the heat to high, add the wine and boil for 1 minute.

4 Add the chopped tomatoes, tomato paste and stock and simmer for 10 minutes. Stir in the cayenne pepper, peas and meatballs and simmer for 5–10 minutes, or until the sauce is thick. Serve hot.

MAINS

CABBAGE ROLLS

MAKES 12 LARGE ROLLS

1 tablespoon olive oil

1 onion, finely chopped

large pinch of allspice

1 teaspoon ground cumin

large pinch of ground nutmeg

2 bay leaves

1 large head of cabbage

500 g (1 lb 2 oz) minced (ground) lamb

250 g (9 oz/1 cup) short-grain white rice

4 garlic cloves, crushed

50 g (2 oz/⅓ cup) toasted pine nuts

2 tablespoons chopped mint

2 tablespoons chopped flat-leaf (Italian) parsley

1 tablespoon chopped currants

250 ml (9 fl oz/1 cup) olive oil, extra

80 ml (3 fl oz/⅓ cup) lemon juice

extra virgin olive oil, to drizzle

1 teaspoon salt

lemon wedges, for serving

1   **Heat the oil in a saucepan,** add the onion and cook over medium heat for 10 minutes, or until golden. Add the allspice, cumin and nutmeg, and cook for 2 minutes, or until fragrant. Remove from the pan.

2   **Bring a large saucepan** of water to the boil and add the bay leaves. Cut the tough outer leaves and about 5 cm (2 inch) of the core from the cabbage and add to the saucepan. Cook for 5 minutes, then carefully loosen a whole leaf with tongs and remove. Continue to cook and remove leaves until you reach the core. Drain, reserving cooking liquid. Leave to cool.

3   **Using 12 leaves of equal size** and cut a small 'V' from the core end of each to remove the thickest part. Trim the firm central veins so that the leaf is as flat as possible. Place three-quarters of the remaining leaves on the base of a large saucepan to prevent the rolls catching.

4   **Combine minced meat,** onion mixture, rice, garlic, pine nuts, mint, parsley and currants in a bowl and season well. With the core end of a leaf closest to you, form 2 tablespoons of mixture into an oval and place in the centre of the leaf. Roll up, tucking in the sides. Repeat with the remaining 11 leaves and filling. Place tightly, in a single layer, in the lined saucepan, seam-side-down.

5   **Combine 625 ml** (22 fl oz/2½ cups) of the cooking liquid with the extra olive oil, lemon juice and salt, and pour over the rolls (the liquid should just come to the top of the rolls). Lay the remaining cabbage leaves over the top. Cover and bring to the boil over high heat, then reduce the heat and simmer for 1 hour 15 minutes, or until the mince and rice are cooked. Carefully remove from the pan with a slotted spoon, then drizzle with extra virgin olive oil. Serve with lemon wedges.

LENTIL AND BURGHUL FRITTERS

MAKES 35

140 g (5 oz/¾ cup) brown lentils, rinsed

90 g (3 oz/½ cup) burghul (bulgur)

80 ml (3 fl oz/⅓ cup) olive oil

1 onion, finely chopped

2 garlic cloves, finely chopped

3 teaspoons ground cumin

2 teaspoons ground coriander

3 tablespoons finely chopped mint

4 eggs, lightly beaten

60 g (2 oz/½ cup) plain (all-purpose) flour

1 teaspoon sea salt

YOGHURT SAUCE

1 small Lebanese (short) cucumber, peeled

250 g (9 oz/1 cup) Greek-style natural yoghurt

1–2 garlic cloves, crushed

1 Place the lentils in a saucepan with 625 ml (22 fl oz/ 2½ cups) water. Bring to the boil over high heat, then reduce the heat and simmer for 30 minutes, or until tender. Remove from the heat and top up with enough water to just cover the lentils. Pour in burghul, cover and leave to stand for 1½ hours, or until the burghul has expanded.

2 For the yoghurt sauce, halve the cucumber lengthways, remove the seeds with a teaspoon and discard. Grate the flesh and mix in a bowl with the yoghurt and garlic.

3 Heat half the oil in a large frying pan over medium heat, add the onion and garlic and cook for 5 minutes, or until soft. Stir in the cumin and coriander. Add the onion mixture, mint, eggs, flour and sea salt to the lentil mixture and mix well. The mixture should hold together enough to drop spoonfuls into the frying pan. If the mixture is too wet, add flour to bind.

4 Heat the remaining oil over medium heat in the cleaned frying pan. Drop heaped tablespoons of mixture into the pan (fritters should be about 5 cm/2 inches in diameter) and cook for 3 minutes each side, or until browned. Drain on crumpled paper towels, season with salt and serve with yoghurt sauce.

FRIED SQUID RINGS

SERVES 4-6

500 g (1 lb 2 oz) cleaned squid tubes

185 g (7 oz/1½ cups) plain (all-purpose) flour

2 teaspoons sweet paprika (pimentón)

olive oil, for deep-frying

lemon wedges, to serve

aïoli, to serve (optional, see recipe on page 15)

1 **Wash the squid tubes** and cut into rings about 1 cm (½ inch) wide. Combine the flour and paprika.

2 **Season rings** well with salt and pepper and toss in the flour to lightly coat.

3 **Fill a deep, heavy-based saucepan** one-third full of oil and heat to 180°C (350°F), or until a cube of bread dropped into the oil browns in 15 seconds.

4 **Add the squid rings** in batches and cook for 2 minutes, or until golden. Drain well on paper towels and serve hot with the lemon wedges and aïoli, if desired.

MUSSELS SAGANAKI

SERVES 6

750 g (1 lb 10 oz) black mussels

125 ml (4 fl oz/½ cup) dry white wine

3 sprigs of thyme

1 bay leaf

1 tablespoon olive oil

1 large onion, finely chopped

1 garlic clove, finely chopped

420 g (14 oz) ripe tomatoes, peeled and very finely chopped

2 tablespoons tomato paste (concentrated purée)

½ teaspoon sugar

1 tablespoon red wine vinegar

70 g (2 oz) Greek feta cheese, crumbled

1 teaspoon thyme leaves

1 **Scrub the mussels** with a stiff brush and pull out the hairy beards. Discard any broken mussels, or open ones that don't close when tapped on the bench. Rinse well.

2 **Bring the wine,** thyme and bay leaf to the boil in a large pan, add the mussels and cook for 4–5 minutes, or until just opened. Pour the mussel liquid through a strainer into a heatproof bowl and reserve. Discard any unopened mussels. Remove the top half shell from each mussel and discard.

3 **Heat oil in a saucepan,** add onion and stir over medium heat for 3 minutes. Add garlic and cook for 1 minute, or until turning golden. Pour in the reserved mussel liquid, increase the heat and bring to the boil, then boil for 2 minutes, or until almost dry. Add the tomato, tomato paste and sugar, then reduce the heat and simmer for 5 minutes. Add the vinegar and simmer for another 5 minutes.

4 **Add mussels to the pan** and cook over medium heat for 1 minute, or until heated through. Spoon into a warm serving dish. Top with crumbled feta and the thyme leaves. Serve hot.

Note: Saganaki refers to the utensil used to cook the food in. It is a frying pan with two handles, used for cooking a range of meze as it can be transferred from stovetop to table. Any pan of a suitable size can be used.

KAKAVIA

SERVES 6

2 onions, finely sliced

400 g (14 oz) tin chopped tomatoes

750 g (1 lb 10 oz) potatoes, cut into
  5 mm (¼ inch) slices

1 teaspoon chopped oregano

150 ml (5 fl oz) olive oil

2 litres (70 fl oz/8 cups) fish or vegetable
  stock

1.5 kg (3 lb 5 oz) white fish fillets, such
  as cod, jewfish or snapper, cut into
  chunks

500 g (1 lb 2 oz) raw prawn (shrimp)
  meat

125 ml (4 fl oz/½ cup) lemon juice

chopped flat-leaf parsley, to garnish

1 Layer the onion, tomato and potato in a large heavy-based saucepan, seasoning with salt, pepper and oregano between each layer. Add oil and stock and bring the mixture to the boil. Reduce the heat and simmer for 10 minutes, or until the potato is cooked through and tender.

2 Add the fish and prawn meat and cook for 5 minutes, or until the seafood is cooked. Add the juice, spoon into bowls and top with parsley.

BAKED FISH WITH TOMATO AND O.

SERVES 4

60 ml (2 fl oz/¼ cup) olive oil

2 onions, finely chopped

1 small celery stalk, finely chopped

1 small carrot, finely chopped

2 garlic cloves, chopped

400 g (14 oz) tin chopped tomatoes

2 tablespoons tomato passata (puréed tomatoes)

¼ teaspoon dried oregano

½ teaspoon sugar

50 g (2 oz) white bread, preferably one day old

500 g (1 lb 2 oz) white fish fillets or steaks, such as snapper or cod

3 tablespoons chopped flat-leaf (Italian) parsley

1 tablespoon fresh lemon juice

1 Preheat oven to 180°C (350°F/Gas 4). Heat 2 tablespoons of the oil in a heavy-based frying pan. Add the onion, celery and carrot and cook over low heat for 10 minutes, or until soft. Add garlic, cook for 2 minutes, then add the chopped tomato, passata, oregano and sugar. Simmer for about 10 minutes, stirring occasionally, until reduced and thickened. Season.

2 To make the breadcrumbs, chop the bread in a food processor for a few minutes, until fine crumbs form.

3 Arrange fish pieces in a single layer in a baking dish. Stir the chopped parsley and the lemon juice into the sauce. Season, to taste, and pour over the fish. Scatter the breadcrumbs over the top and drizzle with remaining oil. Bake for 20 minutes, or until the fish is just cooked.

AVGOLEMONO SOUP WITH CHICKEN

SERVES 4

1 onion, halved

2 cloves

1 carrot, cut into chunks

1 bay leaf

500 g (1 lb 2 oz) boneless, skinless chicken breasts

75 g (3 oz/⅓ cup) short-grain rice

3 eggs, separated

3 tablespoons lemon juice

2 tablespoons chopped flat-leaf (Italian) parsley

4 thin lemon slices, to garnish

1 Stud the onion with the cloves and place in a large saucepan with 1.5 litres (52 fl oz/6 cups) water. Add the carrot, bay leaf and chicken and season with salt and freshly ground black pepper. Slowly bring to the boil, then reduce the heat and simmer for 10 minutes, or until the chicken is cooked.

2 Strain the stock into a clean saucepan, reserving the chicken and discarding the vegetables. Add the rice to the stock, bring to the boil, then reduce the heat and simmer for 15 minutes, or until the rice is tender. Meanwhile, tear the chicken into shreds.

3 Whisk egg whites in a clean dry bowl until stiff peaks form, then beat in the yolks. Slowly beat in the lemon juice. Gently stir in about 150 ml (5 fl oz) of the hot (not boiling) stock and beat thoroughly. Add the egg mixture to the stock and heat gently, but do not let it boil otherwise the eggs may scramble. Add the chicken and season with salt and black pepper.

4 Set aside for 2–3 minutes to allow flavours to develop, then sprinkle on the parsley. Garnish with lemon slices and serve with plenty of crusty bread and a green salad.

LEMONY CHICKEN

SERVES 4

3 tablespoons olive oil

1 kg (2 lb 4 oz) chicken drumsticks, seasoned

1 large leek, halved, washed and thinly sliced

4 large strips lemon zest, white pith removed

125 ml (4 fl oz/½ cup) fresh lemon juice

250 ml (9 fl oz/1 cup) dry white wine

500 g (1 lb 2 oz) baby carrots, trimmed

1 **In a large heavy-based frying pan,** heat the oil and sauté the chicken in two batches, for 6–8 minutes each batch, or until brown and crispy. Return all the chicken to the pan, add the leek and cook until the leek is just wilted. Add the lemon zest and cook for 1–2 minutes.

2 **Pour the lemon juice** and wine into the pan and allow the flavours to combine for a few seconds. Stir, add the carrots, then cover and cook for 30–35 minutes, stirring occasionally, until the chicken is cooked. Remove the zest, then taste and adjust the seasoning if necessary.

:D BEEF AND ONIONS

SERVES 4

1 kg (2 lb 4 oz) chuck steak

60 ml (2 fl oz/¼ cup) olive oil

750 g (1 lb 10 oz) whole baby onions

3 garlic cloves, cut in half lengthways

125 ml (4 fl oz½ cup) red wine

1 cinnamon stick

4 whole cloves

1 bay leaf

1 tablespoon red wine vinegar

2 tablespoons tomato paste
    (concentrated purée)

¼ teaspoon cracked black pepper

2 tablespoons currants

1 **Trim the meat** of excess fat and sinew, then cut into bite-sized cubes. Heat the oil over medium heat in a large heavy-based saucepan. Add the onions and stir for 5 minutes, or until golden. Remove from the pan and drain on paper towels.

2 **Add the meat** all at once to the pan and stir over high heat for 10 minutes, or until the meat is well browned and almost all the liquid has been absorbed.

3 **Add the garlic,** wine, spices, bay leaf, vinegar, tomato paste, black pepper, some salt and 375 ml (13 fl oz/1½ cups) water to the pan and bring to the boil. Reduce the heat, cover and simmer for 1 hour, stirring occasionally.

4 **Return the onions** to the pan, add the currants and stir gently. Simmer, covered, for 15 minutes. Discard cinnamon before serving. Serve with rice, bread or potatoes.

Note: For a richer flavour, use 375 ml (13 fl oz/1½ cups) beef or veal stock instead of water in this recipe, or 250 ml (9 fl oz/1 cup) each of wine and water.

SOUVLAKI

SERVES 4

1 kg (2 lb 4 oz) boned leg lamb, trimmed, cut into 2 cm (¾ inch) cubes

60 ml (2 fl oz/¼ cup olive oil

2 teaspoons finely grated lemon zest

80 ml (3 fl oz/⅓ cup) lemon juice

125 ml (4 fl oz/½ cup) dry white wine

2 teaspoons dried oregano

2 large garlic cloves, finely chopped

2 bay leaves

250 g (9 oz/1 cup) Greek-style natural yoghurt

2 garlic cloves, crushed, extra

1 **Place lamb** in a non-metallic bowl with 2 tablespoons oil, the lemon zest and juice, wine, oregano, garlic, bay leaves and some black pepper. Toss, then cover and refrigerate overnight.

2 **Place the yoghurt** and extra garlic in a bowl, mix well and leave for 30 minutes.

3 **Drain the lamb.** Thread onto 8 skewers and cook on a barbecue or chargrill plate, brushing with the remaining oil, for 7–8 minutes, or until done to your liking. Serve with the yoghurt, bread and a salad.

MOUSSAKA

SERVES 6

1.5 kg (3 lb 5 oz) eggplants (aubergines),
  cut into 5 mm (¼ inch) slices

125 ml (4 fl oz/½ cup) olive oil

2 onions, finely chopped

2 large cloves garlic, crushed

½ teaspoon ground allspice

1 teaspoon ground cinnamon

750 g (1 lb 10 oz/) minced (ground)
  lamb

2 large ripe tomatoes, peeled and
  chopped

2 tablespoons tomato paste (tomato
  purée)

125 ml (4 fl oz/½ cup) white wine

3 tablespoons chopped flat-leaf parsley

CHEESE SAUCE

60 g (2 oz) butter

60 g (2 oz/½ cup) plain (all-purpose)
  flour

625 ml (22 fl oz/2½ cups) milk

pinch of ground nutmeg

35 g (1 oz/⅓ cup) finely grated kefalotyri
  or parmesan cheese

2 eggs, lightly beaten

1   **Lay eggplant on a tray,** sprinkle with salt and leave to stand for 30 minutes. Rinse under water and pat dry. Preheat the oven to 180°C (350°F/Gas 4).

2   **Heat 2 tablespoons olive oil** in a frying pan, add the eggplant in batches and cook for 1–2 minutes each side, or until golden and soft. Add a little more oil when needed.

3   **Heat 1 tablespoon** olive oil in a large saucepan, add the onion and cook over medium heat for 5 minutes. Add garlic, allspice and cinnamon and cook for 30 seconds. Add the lamb and cook for 5 minutes, or until browned, breaking up lumps with the back of a spoon. Add tomato, tomato paste and wine, and simmer over low heat for 30 minutes, or until the liquid has evaporated. Stir in chopped parsley and season, to taste.

4   **For the cheese sauce,** melt the butter in a saucepan over low heat. Stir in the flour and cook for 1 minute, or until pale and foaming. Remove from the heat and gradually stir in the milk and nutmeg. Return to the heat and stir constantly until the sauce boils and thickens. Reduce the heat and simmer for 2 minutes. Stir in 1 tablespoon of the cheese until well combined. Stir in the egg just before using.

5   **Line the base of a 3 litre** (105 fl oz/12 cup) ovenproof dish measuring 25 x 30 cm (10 x 12 inches) with a third of the eggplant. Spoon half the meat sauce over the top and cover with another layer of eggplant. Spoon remaining meat sauce over the top and cover with the remaining eggplant. Spread cheese sauce over the top and sprinkle with remaining cheese. Bake for 1 hour. Leave to stand for 10 minutes before slicing.

STUFFED CAPSICUMS

SERVES 6

175 g (6 oz) long-grain white rice

315 ml (11 fl oz/1¼ cups) chicken stock

6 medium-sized red, yellow or orange
  capsicums (peppers)

60 g (2 oz) pine nuts

80 ml (3 fl oz/⅓ cup) olive oil

1 large onion, chopped

125 g (4 oz/½ cup) tomato passata
  (puréed tomatoes)

60 g (2 oz) currants

2½ tablespoons chopped flat-leaf
  (Italian) parsley

2½ tablespoons chopped mint leaves

½ teaspoon ground cinnamon

1 Put the rice and stock in a saucepan and bring to the boil over medium heat. Reduce the heat to medium-low, cover tightly and cook for 15 minutes, or until tender. Remove from the heat and set aside, covered.

2 Bring a large saucepan of water to the boil. Cut off the tops of the capsicums, reserving the lids. Remove the seeds and membrane from the capsicums and discard. Blanch the capsicums in the boiling water (not the lids) for 2 minutes, then drain and leave upturned to dry on paper towels.

3 Preheat the oven to 180°C (350°F/Gas 4). Toast the pine nuts in a small frying pan over low heat until golden brown, then remove from the pan and set aside. Increase the heat to medium and heat 2 tablespoons of oil. Add the onion and cook for 10 minutes or until soft, stirring occasionally.

4 Add tomato passata, currants, parsley, mint, cinnamon, cooked rice and toasted pine nuts to the pan. Stir 2 minutes, then season, to taste, with salt and pepper.

5 Stand the capsicums in a baking tray in which they fit snugly. Divide the rice mixture among the capsicum cavities. Replace the lids.

6 Pour 100 ml (4 fl oz) boiling water into the dish and drizzle remaining oil over the top of the capsicums. Bake for 40 minutes, or until capsicums are just tender when tested with the point of a small knife. Serve warm or cold.

CHICKEN PIE

SERVES 6

1 kg (2 lb 4 oz) boneless, skinless chicken breasts

500 ml (17 fl oz/2 cups) chicken stock

60 g (2 oz) butter

2 spring onions (scallions), trimmed and finely chopped

60 g (2 oz/½ cup) plain (all-purpose) flour

125 ml (4 fl oz/½ cup) milk

8 sheets filo pastry (40 x 30 cm/ 16 x 12 inch)

60 g (2 oz) butter, extra, melted

200 g (7 oz) feta cheese, crumbled

1 tablespoon chopped dill

1 tablespoon chopped chives

¼ teaspoon ground nutmeg

1 egg, lightly beaten

1 Cut chicken into bite-sized pieces. Pour stock into a saucepan and bring to the boil over high heat. Reduce the heat to low, add the chicken and poach gently for 10–15 minutes, or until the chicken is cooked through. Drain, reserving the stock. Add water to stock to bring the quantity up to 500 ml (17 fl oz/2 cups). Preheat the oven to 180°C (350°F/Gas 4).

2 Melt the butter in a saucepan over low heat, add the spring onion and cook, stirring, for 5 minutes. Add the flour and stir for 30 seconds. Remove the pan from the heat and gradually add the chicken stock and milk, stirring after each addition. Return to the heat; gently bring to the boil, stirring. Simmer for a few minutes, or until sauce thickens. Remove from the heat.

3 Line a baking dish 25 x 18 x 4 cm (10 x 7 x 1½ inches) with 4 sheets of filo pastry, brushing one side of each sheet with melted butter as you go. Place the buttered side down. The filo will overlap the edges of the dish. Cover the unused filo with a damp tea towel (dish towel) to prevent it drying out.

4 Stir the chicken, cheese, dill, chives, nutmeg and egg into the sauce. Season, to taste, with salt and freshly ground black pepper. Pile the mixture on top of the filo pastry in the dish. Fold the overlapping filo over the filling and cover the top of the pie with the remaining 4 sheets of filo, brushing each sheet with melted butter as you go. Scrunch the edges of the filo so that they fit in the dish. Brush the top with butter. Bake for 45–50 minutes, or until the pastry is golden brown and crisp.

SERVES 4

1.5 kg (3 lb 5 oz) chicken, cut into
  8 even-sized pieces

1 tablespoon olive oil

12 fresh figs (not too big), or 12 dried
  figs, soaked in hot water for 2 hours

10 whole garlic cloves

1 large onion, thinly sliced

½ teaspoon ground coriander

½ teaspoon ground cinnamon

½ teaspoon ground cumin

pinch of cayenne

3 bay leaves

375 ml (13 fl oz/1½ cups) ruby port

1 teaspoon finely grated lemon zest

2 tablespoons lemon juice

1 Preheat the oven to 180°C (350°F/Gas 4). Remove any excess chicken fat. Reserve chicken giblets, if there are any. Lightly season the chicken. Heat the olive oil in a large heavy-based frying pan over high heat. Cook the chicken in batches, skin-side-down, for 5 minutes, or until the skin is golden.

2 Remove from the pan and place skin-side-down in a single layer in a 33 x 23 cm (13 x 9 inch) baking dish with the giblets, if using. Place the figs between the chicken pieces. Scatter the garlic and onion over the top, carefully pressing them into any gaps and being careful not to squash the figs. Sprinkle the spices over the top, tuck in the bay leaves, then pour in the port.

3 Cover and bake chicken for 25 minutes, then turn it over. Uncover and bake for another 20 minutes, or until chicken is just tender. Stir in the lemon zest and juice and bake for another 15 minutes, or until the chicken is very tender.

SPANOKOPITA

SERVES 4–6

1.5 kg (3 lb 5 oz) silverbeet (Swiss chard)

3 tablespoons olive oil

1 white onion, finely chopped

10 spring onions (scallions), chopped (include some green)

1½ tablespoons chopped dill

200 g (7 oz) Greek feta cheese, crumbled

125 g (4 oz) cottage cheese

3 tablespoons finely grated kefalotyri cheese (see Note)

¼ teaspoon ground nutmeg

4 eggs, lightly beaten

10 sheets filo pastry

80 g (3 oz) butter, melted, for brushing

1   Rinse and drain the silverbeet thoroughly. Discard stems and shred the leaves. Heat olive oil in a large frying pan, add the onion and cook, stirring, over medium heat for 5 minutes, or until softened. Add the spring onion and silverbeet and cook, covered, over medium heat for 5 minutes. Add dill and cook, uncovered, for 3–4 minutes, or until most of the liquid has evaporated. Remove from heat; cool to room temperature.

2   Preheat the oven to 180°C (350°F/Gas 4) and lightly grease a 20 x 25 cm (8 x 10 inch) 2.5 litre (87 fl oz/10 cups) baking dish. Place the feta, cottage and kefalotyri cheeses in a large bowl. Stir in the silverbeet mixture and add the nutmeg. Gradually add the eggs and combine well. Season, to taste.

3   Line the base and sides of the baking dish with a sheet of filo pastry. (Keep the rest covered with a damp tea towel to prevent drying out.) Brush with butter and cover with another sheet of filo. Butter the sheet and repeat in this way, using five sheets of pastry. Spoon the filling into the dish and level the surface. Fold the exposed pastry up and over to cover the top of the filling. Cover with a sheet of pastry, brush with butter and continue until all the sheets are used. Roughly trim the pastry with kitchen scissors then tuck the excess inside the wall of the dish.

4   Brush the top with butter. Using a sharp knife, score the surface into squares. Sprinkle a few drops of cold water on the top to help prevent the pastry from curling. Then bake for 45 minutes, or until puffed and golden. Leave at room temperature for 10 minutes before serving.

Note: You can use pecorino cheese if kefalotyri is unavailable.

PASTITSIO

SERVES 6

150 g (5 oz) elbow macaroni

40 g (1½ oz) butter

¼ teaspoon ground nutmeg

60 g (2 oz) kefalotyri or parmesan cheese, grated

1 egg, lightly beaten

MEAT SAUCE

2 tablespoons oil

1 onion, finely chopped

2 garlic cloves, crushed

500 g (1 lb 2 oz) minced (ground) beef

125 ml (4 fl oz/½ cup) red wine

250 ml (9 fl oz/1 cup) beef stock

3 tablespoons tomato paste (concentrated purée)

1 teaspoon chopped oregano

BECHAMEL SAUCE

40 g (1½ oz) butter

1½ tablespoons plain (all-purpose) flour

pinch of nutmeg

375 ml (13 cups/1½ cups) milk

1 egg, lightly beaten

1 Preheat the oven to 180°C (350°F/Gas 4). Lightly grease a 1.5 litre (52 fl oz/6 cups) ovenproof dish. Cook the macaroni in a large saucepan of boiling salted water for 10 minutes, or until al dente. Drain and return to the pan. Melt the butter in a small saucepan until golden, then pour it over the macaroni. Stir in the nutmeg and half the cheese and season, to taste. Leave until cool, then mix in the egg and set aside.

2 For the meat sauce, heat the oil in a large frying pan, add the onion and garlic and cook over medium heat for 6 minutes, or until the onion is soft. Increase the heat, add the beef and cook, stirring, for 5 minutes or until the meat is browned. Add the wine and cook over high heat for 1 minute, or until evaporated. Add the stock, tomato paste, oregano, salt and pepper. Reduce heat, cover and simmer for 20 minutes.

3 Meanwhile, to make the béchamel sauce, melt the butter in a small saucepan over low heat. Stir in the flour and cook for 1 minute, or until pale and foaming. Remove from the heat and gradually stir in the milk. Return to the heat and stir constantly until the sauce boils and thickens. Reduce the heat and simmer for 2 minutes. Add the nutmeg and some salt and pepper. Allow to cool a little before stirring in the beaten egg. Stir 3 tablespoons of the béchamel into the meat sauce.

4 Spread half the meat sauce in the dish, then layer half the pasta over it. Layer with the remaining meat sauce and then the remaining pasta. Press down firmly with the back of a spoon. Spread the béchamel sauce over the pasta and sprinkle the remaining cheese on top. Bake for 45–50 minutes, or until golden. Let it stand for 15 minutes before serving.

OCTOPUS IN RED WINE STEW

SERVES 4–6

1 kg (2 lb 4 oz) baby octopus

2 tablespoons olive oil

1 large onion, chopped

3 garlic cloves, crushed

1 bay leaf

750 ml (25 fl oz/3 cups) red wine

60 ml (2 fl oz/¼ cup) red wine vinegar

400 g (14 oz) tin crushed tomatoes

1 tablespoon tomato paste
(concentrated purée)

1 tablespoon finely chopped oregano

¼ teaspoon ground cinnamon

small pinch of ground cloves

1 teaspoon sugar

2 tablespoons chopped flat-leaf (Italian)
parsley

1   To prepare each octopus, using a small knife, cut between the head and tentacles, just below the eyes. Grasp the body and push the beak out and up through the centre of the tentacles with your fingers. Cut the eyes from the head by slicing a small round off with a small sharp knife. Discard the eye section. Carefully slit through one side of the head and remove any gut from inside. Thoroughly rinse all the octopus under running water.

2   Heat the oil in a large saucepan, add the onion and cook over high heat for 5 minutes, or until starting to brown. Add the garlic and bay leaf and cook for another minute. Add the octopus and stir to thoroughly coat in the onion mixture.

3   Add the wine, vinegar, tomato, tomato paste, oregano, cinnamon, cloves and sugar. Bring to the boil, then reduce the heat to low and simmer for 1 hour, or until the octopus is tender and the sauce has thickened slightly. Stir in the parsley and season.

Note: The cooking time for octopus varies according to the size. Generally the smaller octopus are not as tough as the larger ones and will take less time to cook.

STUFFED SQUID

SERVES 4

TOMATO SAUCE

4 large ripe tomatoes

1 tablespoon olive oil

1 onion, finely chopped

1 garlic cloves, crushed

60 ml (2 fl oz/¼ cup) good-quality red wine

1 tablespoon chopped oregano

STUFFING

1 tablespoon olive oil

2 spring onions (scallions), chopped

280 g (10 oz/1½ cups) cold, cooked rice (see Note)

60 g (2 oz) pine nuts

75 g (3 oz) currants

2 tablespoons chopped flat-leaf (Italian) parsley

2 teaspoons finely grated lemon zest

1 egg, lightly beaten

1 kg (2 lb 4 oz) medium squid tubes

1 Preheat oven to 160°C (315°F/Gas 2–3). For the tomato sauce, score a cross in the base of each tomato, soak them in a bowl of boiling water for 10 seconds, then plunge them into cold water and peel the skin from the cross. Chop the flesh. Heat the oil in a frying pan. Add the onion and garlic and cook over low heat for about 2 minutes, stirring frequently, until the onion is soft. Add the tomato, wine and oregano and bring to the boil. Reduce the heat, then cover and cook over low heat for 10 minutes.

2 Meanwhile, for the stuffing, mix all the ingredients except the egg in a bowl. Add enough egg to moisten the ingredients.

3 Wash squid and pat dry with paper towels. Three-quarters fill each tube with stuffing and secure the ends with toothpicks or skewers. Place in a single layer in a casserole dish.

4 Pour tomato sauce over the squid, cover the dish and bake for 20 minutes, or until the squid are tender. Cut the squid into thick slices. Spoon sauce over just before serving.

Note: You will need to cook 100 g (4 oz/½ cup) rice for this recipe. The cooking time for the squid will depend upon the size. Choose small squid because they are more tender.

BAKED EGGPLANT

SERVES 4

185 ml (6 fl oz/¾ cup) olive oil

1 kg (2 lb 4 oz) elongated eggplants
  (aubergines), cut in half lengthways

3 onions, thinly sliced

3 garlic cloves, finely chopped

400 g (14 oz) roma (plum) tomatoes,
  peeled and chopped, or a 400 g
  (14 oz) tin chopped tomatoes

2 teaspoons dried oregano

4 tablespoons chopped flat-leaf (Italian)
  parsley

35 g (1¼ oz/¼ cup) currants

¼ teaspoon ground cinnamon

2 tablespoons lemon juice

pinch of sugar

125 ml (4 fl oz/½ cup) tomato juice

1 Preheat the oven to 180° (350°F/Gas 4). Heat half the olive oil in a large heavy-based frying pan and cook the eggplants on all sides for about 8–10 minutes, until the cut sides are golden. Remove from the pan and scoop out some of the flesh, leaving the skins intact and some flesh lining the skins. Finely chop the scooped-out flesh and set aside.

2 Heat the remaining olive oil in the same frying pan and cook the onion over medium heat for 8–10 minutes, until transparent. Add the garlic and cook for another minute. Add the tomato, oregano, parsley, currants, cinnamon, reserved eggplant flesh and salt and pepper, to taste.

3 Place the eggplant shells in a large ovenproof dish and fill each with tomato mixture.

4 Mix the lemon juice, sugar, tomato juice and some salt and pour over the eggplant. Cover and bake for 30 minutes, then uncover and cook for another 10 minutes. To serve, place on a serving platter and lightly drizzle with any remaining juice.

GREAT TASTES MEDITERRANEAN

ZUCCHINI PATTIES

300 g (11 oz) zucchini (courgettes), grated

1 small onion, finely chopped

30 g (1 oz/¼ cup) self-raising flour

35 g (1¼ oz/⅓ cup) grated kefalotyri or parmesan cheese

1 tablespoon chopped mint

2 teaspoons chopped flat-leaf (Italian) parsley

pinch of ground nutmeg

25 g (¾ oz/¼ cup) dry breadcrumbs

1 egg, lightly beaten

1   Put zucchini and onion in the centre of a clean tea towel (dish towel), gather the corners together and twist as tightly as possible to remove all the juices. Combine the zucchini, onion, flour, cheese, mint, parsley, nutmeg, breadcrumbs and egg in a large bowl. Season well with salt and cracked black pepper. Mix with your hands into a stiff mixture that clumps together.

2   Heat the oil in a large frying pan over medium heat. When hot, drop level tablespoons of mixture into the pan and shallow-fry for 2–3 minutes, or until well browned all over. Drain well on crumpled paper towels and serve hot, with lemon wedges, or with cucumber and yoghurt salad.

BRAISED LAMB SHANKS WITH HARICOT BEANS

SERVES 4

400 g (14 oz/2 cups) dried haricot beans

4 tablespoons oil

4 lamb shanks, trimmed

2 tablespoons butter

2 garlic cloves, crushed

2 brown onions, finely chopped

1½ tablespoons thyme

2 tablespoons tomato paste
(concentrated purée)

2 x 400 g (14 oz) tins crushed tomatoes

1 tablespoon paprika

1 dried jalapeño chilli, roughly chopped

30 g (1 oz/1 cup) roughly chopped flat-
leaf (Italian) parsley

1   Put the haricot beans in a bowl, cover with water and soak overnight.

2   Heat 3 tablespoons of the oil in a large heavy-based frying pan over medium heat and brown the shanks on all sides. Remove and set aside. Drain the fat from the pan.

3   Heat the butter and the remaining oil in the pan and cook the garlic and onion over medium heat for 3–4 minutes, or until softened. Add the thyme, tomato paste, tomato and paprika and simmer for 5 minutes. Add the lamb shanks and 500 ml (17 fl oz/2 cups) hot water. Season well and bring to the boil. Cover the pan, reduce the heat and simmer gently for 30 minutes.

4   Drain the beans and add to the pan with the jalapeño chilli and another 500 ml (17 fl oz/2 cups) of hot water. Bring to the boil again, cover and simmer for another 1–1½ hours or until both the beans and the meat are tender, adding more water, 125 ml (4 fl oz/½ cup) at a time, if necessary. Check the seasoning, adjust if necessary, and stir in half the parsley. Serve hot sprinkled with the remaining parsley.

LAMB KEFTA

SERVES 4

1 kg (2 lb 4 oz) minced (ground) lamb

1 onion, finely chopped

2 garlic cloves, finely chopped

2 tablespoons finely chopped flat-leaf (Italian) parsley

2 tablespoons finely chopped coriander (cilantro) leaves

½ teaspoon cayenne pepper

½ teaspoon allspice

½ teaspoon ground ginger

½ teaspoon ground cardamom

1 teaspoon ground cumin

1 teaspoon paprika

SAUCE

2 tablespoons olive oil

1 onion, finely chopped

2 garlic cloves, finely chopped

2 teaspoons ground cumin

½ teaspoon ground cinnamon

1 teaspoon paprika

2 x 400 g (14 oz) tins chopped tomatoes

2 teaspoons harissa

4 tablespoons chopped coriander (cilantro) leaves

1 Preheat the oven to 180°C (350°F/Gas 4). Lightly grease two baking trays. Place the lamb, onion, garlic, parsley, coriander, cayenne, allspice, ginger, cardamom, cumin and paprika in a bowl and mix well. Season well. Roll rounded tablespoons of the mixture into balls and place on the trays. Bake for 18–20 minutes, or until browned.

2 Meanwhile, for the sauce, heat the oil in a large saucepan, add the onion and cook over medium heat for 5 minutes, or until soft. Add the garlic, cumin, cinnamon and paprika, and cook for 1 minute, or until fragrant.

3 Stir in the tomato and harissa and bring to the boil. Reduce the heat to low and simmer for 20 minutes, then add the meatballs and simmer for 10 minutes, or until warmed through. Stir in the coriander, season well and serve.

LAMB PILAF

SERVES 4–6

1 large eggplant (aubergine), about 500 g (1 lb 2 oz), cut into 1 cm (½ in) cubes

125 ml (4 fl oz/½ cup) olive oil

1 large onion, finely chopped

2 teaspoons ground cumin

1 teaspoon ground cinnamon

1 teaspoon ground coriander

300 g (11 oz) long-grain rice

500 ml (17 fl oz/2 cups) chicken or vegetable stock

500 g (1 lb 2 oz) minced (ground) lamb

½ teaspoon allspice

2 tablespoons olive oil, extra

2 vine-ripened tomatoes, cut into wedges

3 tablespoons toasted pistachios

2 tablespoons currants

2 tablespoons chopped coriander (cilantro) leaves, to garnish

1 **Place the eggplant in a colander,** sprinkle generously with salt and leave for 1 hour. Rinse well and squeeze dry in a clean tea towel. Heat 2 tablespoons oil in a large, deep frying pan with a lid, add the eggplant and cook over medium heat for 8–10 minutes, or until golden and cooked through. Drain on paper towels.

2 **Heat the remaining oil,** add the onion and cook for 4–5 minutes, or until soft but not brown. Stir in half of each of the cumin, cinnamon and ground coriander. Add the rice and stir to coat, then add the stock, season and bring to the boil. Reduce the heat and simmer, covered, for 15 minutes, adding a little more water if it starts to dry out.

3 **Meanwhile,** place the lamb in a bowl with the allspice and the remaining cumin, cinnamon and coriander. Season and mix well. Roll into balls the size of macadamia nuts. Heat the extra oil in the frying pan and cook the meatballs in batches over medium heat for 5 minutes each batch, or until lightly browned and cooked through. Drain on paper towels. Add the tomato to the pan and cook, turning, for 3–5 minutes, or until lightly golden. Remove from the pan.

4 **Stir the eggplant,** pistachios, currants and meatballs through the rice (this should be quite dry by now). Serve surrounded by the cooked tomato and garnished with the coriander leaves.

GREAT TASTES MEDITERRANEAN

TURKISH PIZZA

MAKES 8

1 teaspoon dried yeast

½ teaspoon sugar

225 g (8 oz) plain (all-purpose) flour

4 tablespoons olive oil

250 g (9 oz) onions, finely chopped

500 g (1 lb 2 oz) minced (ground) lamb

2 garlic cloves

1 teaspoon ground cinnamon

1½ teaspoons ground cumin

½ teaspoon cayenne pepper

3 tablespoons tomato paste
(concentrated purée)

400 g (14 oz) tin crushed tomatoes

50 g (2 oz/⅓ cup) pine nuts

3 tablespoons chopped coriander
(cilantro) leaves

Greek-style natural yoghurt, for serving

1   Mix the yeast, sugar and 60 ml (2 fl oz/¼ cup) warm water in a bowl. Leave in a warm place for 20 minutes, or until bubbles appear on the surface. The mixture should be frothy and increased in volume.

2   Sift flour and 1 teaspoon salt into a bowl, stir in the yeast mixture, 1 tablespoon oil and 100 ml (3 fl oz) warm water. Mix to form a soft dough. Turn onto a floured board and knead for 10 minutes, or until smooth. Place in an oiled bowl, cover and leave in a warm place for 1 hour, or until doubled in size.

3   Heat 2 tablespoons oil in a frying pan over a low heat and cook onion for 5 minutes, or until soft but not golden. Add the lamb and cook for 10 minutes, or until brown. Add the garlic and spices, tomato paste and tomato. Cook 15 minutes, until

quite dry. Add half the pine nuts and 2 tablespoons coriander. Season, then leave to cool. Preheat the oven to 210°C (415°F/Gas 6–7). Grease two baking trays.

4   Knock down the dough, then turn out onto a floured surface. Form into 8 portions and roll each into an 18 x 12 cm (7 x 5 inch) oval. Place on the trays. Divide the lamb among them and spread, leaving a small border. Sprinkle with pine nuts. Brush the edges with oil. Roll the uncovered dough over to cover the outer edges of the filling. Pinch the sides together at each end. Brush with oil. Bake for 15 minutes, or until golden. Sprinkle with coriander and serve with yoghurt.

MINESTRONE WITH PESTO

SERVES 6

125 g (4 oz) dried borlotti beans

60 ml (2 fl oz/¼ cup) olive oil

1 large onion, finely chopped

2 garlic cloves, crushed

60 g (2 oz) pancetta, finely chopped

1 celery stalk, halved lengthways, then cut into 1 cm (½ inch) slices

1 carrot, halved lengthways, then cut into 1 cm (½ inch) slices

1 potato, diced

2 teaspoons tomato paste (concentrated purée)

400 g (14 oz) tin crushed tomatoes

6 basil leaves, roughly torn

2 litres (70 fl oz/8 cups) chicken or vegetable stock

2 thin zucchini (courgettes), cut into 1.5 cm (½ inch) slices

115 g (4 oz/¾ cup) shelled fresh peas

60 g (2 oz) green beans, cut into short lengths

80 g (3 oz) silverbeet (Swiss chard) leaves, shredded

3 tablespoons chopped flat-leaf (Italian) parsley

75 g (3 oz) ditalini or other small pasta

shop-bought pesto, to serve

1   Soak the borlotti beans in plenty of cold water overnight. Drain and rinse thoroughly under cold water.

2   Heat the oil in a large deep saucepan, add onion, garlic and pancetta and cook over low heat, stirring occasionally, for 8–10 minutes, until softened.

3   Add the celery, carrot and potato to the saucepan and cook for 5 minutes. Stir in the tomato paste, tomato, basil and drained borlotti beans. Season, to taste, with freshly ground black pepper. Add stock and bring slowly to the boil. Cover and simmer, stirring occasionally, for 1 hour 30 minutes.

4   Add remaining vegetables, parsley and pasta. Simmer for 8–10 minutes, or until the vegetables and pasta are just tender. Check for seasoning and adjust if necessary. Spoon the pesto on top of the soup and serve.

TOMATO BREAD SOUP

750 g (1 lb 10 oz) vine-ripened tomatoes

1 loaf (450 g/16 oz) day-old crusty Italian bread

1 tablespoon olive oil

3 garlic cloves, crushed

1 tablespoon tomato paste (concentrated purée)

1.25 litres (44 fl oz/5 cups) hot vegetable stock or water

1 large handful torn basil leaves

2–3 tablespoons extra virgin olive oil

extra virgin olive oil, extra, for serving

1   Score a cross in the base of each tomato, then place the tomatoes in a bowl of boiling water for 20 seconds. Plunge them into cold water. Peel skin away from the cross. Cut tomatoes in half and scoop out seeds with a teaspoon. Roughly chop the tomato flesh.

2   Discard most of the crust from the bread and tear the bread roughly into 3 cm (1 inch) pieces.

3   Heat the oil in a large saucepan. Add the garlic, tomato and tomato paste, then reduce the heat and simmer, stirring occasionally, for 10–15 minutes, or until reduced. Add stock and bring to the boil, stirring for 2–3 minutes. Reduce heat to medium, add bread pieces and cook, stirring, for 5 minutes, or until bread softens and absorbs most of the liquid. Add more stock or water if the soup is too thick. Remove the saucepan from the heat.

4   Stir in the basil leaves and extra virgin olive oil, and leave for 5 minutes so flavours have time to develop. Serve drizzled with a little extra virgin olive oil. Serve with a crisp green salad.

SEAFOOD SALAD

SERVES 4

500 g (1 lb 2 oz) small squid

1 kg (2 lb 4 oz) large clams

1 kg (2 lb 4 oz) mussels

5 tablespoons chopped flat-leaf (Italian)
    parsley (reserve the stalks)

500 g (1 lb 2 oz) raw medium prawns
    (shrimp), peeled, deveined, tails intact

2 tablespoons lemon juice

80 ml (3 fl oz/⅓ cup) olive oil

1 garlic clove, crushed

1 **Grasp each squid body** in one hand and the head and tentacles in the other. Pull to separate. Cut the tentacles from each head below the eyes. Discard the heads. Push out the beaks and discard. Pull the quill from inside each body and discard. Under cold running water, pull away the skin (the flaps can be used). Rinse, then slice into 7 mm (¼ inch) rings.

2 **Scrub the clams and mussels** with a stiff brush and remove the hairy beards. Discard any that are cracked or don't close when tapped. Rinse under cold water. Fill a wide shallow pan with 1 cm (½ inch) water, add the parsley stalks, cover the pan and bring the water to simmering point. Add the clams and mussels in batches, being careful not to overcrowd the pan. Cover and steam over high heat for 2–3 minutes, or until the shells begin to open. Remove with a slotted spoon and place in a colander over a bowl. Return any drained juices to

the pan before cooking the next batch. Continue until all the clams and mussels are cooked. Reserve the cooking liquid. Allow the clams and mussels to cool before removing them from the shells. Discard any unopened ones.

3 **Add 1 litre (35 fl oz/4 cups)** water to the pan with the cooking liquid. Bring to the boil, then add the prawns and cook for 3–4 minutes, or until the water returns to the boil. Remove with a slotted spoon; drain in a colander. Add the squid and cook for 30–40 seconds, until the flesh becomes white and opaque. Remove immediately and drain.

4 **Whisk lemon juice,** oil and garlic in a bowl, then season. Pour over the seafood with 4 tablespoons parsley, then toss. Adjust the seasoning if necessary. Marinate for 30–40 minutes to allow the flavours to develop. Sprinkle with parsley. Serve with crusty bread.

SPICY SEAFOOD SOUP

SERVES 6–8

300 g (11 oz) red mullet fillets

400 g (14 oz) firm white fish fillets

300 g (11 oz) cleaned squid tubes

1½ litres (52 fl oz/6 cups) fish stock

80 ml (3 fl oz/⅓ cup) olive oil

1 white onion, chopped

6 garlic cloves, chopped

1 small red chilli, chopped

1 teaspoon sweet paprika (pimentón)

pinch of saffron threads

150 ml (5 fl oz) white wine

400 g (14 oz) tinned chopped tomatoes

16 raw prawns (shrimp), peeled and
    deveined, tails intact

2 tablespoons brandy

24 black mussels, cleaned

1 tablespoon chopped flat-leaf (Italian)
    parsley, to garnish

PICADA

2 tablespoons olive oil

2 slices day-old bread, cubed

2 garlic cloves

5 whole blanched almonds, toasted

2 tablespoons flat-leaf (Italian) parsley

1 Cut the fish and squid into 4 cm (1½ inch) pieces and refrigerate (until ready to use). Pour the stock into a large saucepan, bring to the boil and boil for 15–20 minutes, or until reduced by half.

2 To make the picada, heat the olive oil in a frying pan, add the bread and stir for 2–3 minutes, or until golden, adding the garlic for the last minute. Process the bread, garlic, almonds and parsley in a food processor and add enough of the stock to make a smooth paste.

3 Heat 2 tablespoons of the oil in a large saucepan, add the onion, garlic, chilli and paprika, and cook, stirring, for 1 minute. Add the saffron, white wine, tomato and remaining stock. Bring to the boil, then reduce the heat and leave to simmer.

4 Heat remaining oil in another frying pan over medium heat and cook fish and squid for 3–5 minutes or until just opaque. Remove and set aside. Add prawns, cook for 1 minute, then pour in the brandy. Add the prawn mixture to the fish.

5 Add mussels to the hot stock and simmer, covered, for 3–5 minutes, or until opened. Discard any that do not open. Return all the seafood to the pan, add the picada, and stir until the sauce has thickened slightly and the seafood is cooked through. Season to taste. Serve garnished with parsley.

LINGUINE PESTO

SERVES 4–6

100 g (4 oz/2 cups) fresh basil leaves

2 garlic cloves, crushed

40 g (1½ oz/¼ cup) pine nuts, toasted

185 ml (6 fl oz/¾ cup) olive oil

50 g (2 oz/½ cup) grated parmesan cheese

500 g (1 lb 2 oz) linguine

shaved or grated parmesan cheese, extra, for serving

1   Finely chop the basil, garlic and pine nuts together in a food processor. With the motor running, add the oil in a steady stream until mixed to a smooth paste. Transfer to a bowl, stir in the Parmesan and season, to taste.

2   Cook the pasta in a large saucepan of rapidly boiling salted water until just tender. Drain well and return to the pan. Toss enough of the pesto through the pasta to coat it well. Serve sprinkled with parmesan.

Note: Refrigerate any leftover pesto in an airtight jar for up to 1 week, first covering the surface with a thin layer of olive oil. Pesto can be frozen for up to a month.

PIZZA RUSTICA

SERVES 6

PASTRY

375 g (13 oz/3 cups) plain (all-purpose) flour

1 teaspoon icing (confectioners') sugar

1 teaspoon salt

155 g (6 oz) butter, chilled and chopped

1 egg

1 egg yolk

2 tablespoons iced water

FILLING

500 g (1 lb 2 oz/2 cups) ricotta cheese

6 eggs, separated

100 g (4 oz) lean bacon, cut into small strips

75 g (3 oz) thickly sliced Milano salami, cut into 5 mm (¼ inch) cubes

100 g (4 oz) mozzarella cheese, grated

100 g (4 oz) smoked mozzarella or other naturally smoked cheese, cut into 1 cm (½ inch) cubes

25 g (1 oz/¼ cup) freshly grated parmesan cheese

1 tablespoon chopped flat-leaf (Italian) parsley

½ teaspoon chopped oregano

pinch of nutmeg

1 egg beaten with 1 tablespoon cold water, for glazing

1 For the pastry, sift the flour, icing sugar and salt into a bowl. Rub in the butter with your fingertips until the mixture resembles fine breadcrumbs. Add the egg and yolk and the water, ½ teaspoon at a time, cutting in with a flat-bladed knife, to form a dough. Turn out onto a lightly floured surface and gather together into a smooth ball. Cover with plastic wrap and refrigerate for 30 minutes.

2 Preheat the oven to 190°C (375°F/Gas 5) and place a baking tray on the centre shelf. Grease a 23 x 25 x 4 cm (9 x 10 x 1½ inch) pie dish.

3 To make filling, place ricotta in a large bowl; beat until smooth. Gradually add egg yolks, beating well after each addition. Add bacon, salami, mozzarella cheeses, parmesan cheese, parsley, oregano and nutmeg. Season well. Beat egg whites in a large bowl until stiff; fold through ricotta mixture.

4 Divide the pastry into two portions, one slightly larger than the other. Roll out the larger portion on a lightly floured surface to a size big enough to fit the base and sides of the dish. Line the dish. Roll out the second pastry portion to the same thickness for the pie lid. Spread the filling over the base and smooth the surface. Brush pastry edges with the egg glaze and position the lid on top. Press edges together firmly then trim with a sharp knife. Press a fluted pattern around the rim with your fingers. Brush the surface well with the egg glaze then prick all over with a fork.

5 Place pie dish on the heated tray. Bake for 45–50 minutes, until the pastry is golden and the filling is set. Cover top loosely with foil if it is browning too quickly. Set aside for 20 minutes before serving.

...AGHETTI PUTTANESCA

SERVES 6

80 ml (3 fl oz/⅓ cup) olive oil

2 onions, finely chopped

3 garlic cloves, finely chopped

½ teaspoon chilli flakes

6 large ripe tomatoes, diced

4 tablespoons capers, rinsed

8 anchovies in oil, drained, chopped

150 g (6 oz) kalamata olives

3 tablespoons chopped flat-leaf (Italian) parsley

375 g (13 oz) spaghetti

1   Heat the olive oil in a saucepan, add the onion and cook over medium heat for 5 minutes. Add the garlic and the chilli flakes to the pan and cook for 30 seconds. Add tomato, capers and anchovies. Simmer over low heat for 10–15 minutes, or until the sauce is thick and pulpy. Stir the olives and parsley through the sauce.

2   While the sauce is cooking, cook the spaghetti in a large saucepan of rapidly boiling salted water until al dente. Drain and return to the pan.

3   Add the sauce to the pasta and stir it through. Season with salt and freshly ground black pepper, to taste, and serve immediately.

BUCATINI ALLA NORMA

SERVES 4–6

185 ml (6 fl oz/¾ cup) olive oil

1 brown onion, finely chopped

2 garlic cloves, crushed

2 x 400 g (14 oz) tins crushed tomatoes

1 large eggplant (aubergine), about
    500 g (1 lb 2 oz)

1 large hangeful fresh basil leaves, torn

400 g (14 oz) bucatini

60 g (2 oz/½ cup) ricotta salata
    (see Note), crumbled

50 g (2 oz/½ cup) grated pecorino or
    parmesan cheese

1 tablespoon extra virgin olive oil

1 Heat 2 tablespoons of the oil in a heavy-based frying pan and cook the onion over moderate heat for 5 minutes, or until softened. Add the garlic to the pan and cook for another 30 seconds. Add the tomato and salt and pepper, to taste, and reduce the heat. Cook for 20–25 minutes, or until the sauce has thickened and reduced.

2 While the sauce is cooking, cut the eggplant lengthways into 5 mm (¼ inch) thick slices. Heat the remaining olive oil in a large heavy-based frying pan. When the oil is hot but not smoking, add the eggplant slices a few at a time and cook for 3–5 minutes, or until lightly browned on both sides. Remove from the pan and drain well on crumpled paper towels.

3 Cut each slice of eggplant into 3 pieces and add to the tomato sauce with the torn basil. Stir and keep warm over very low heat.

4 Cook the bucatini in a large saucepan of rapidly boiling, salted water until al dente. Drain well and add to the tomato sauce with half each of the ricotta and pecorino. Toss well and serve immediately sprinkled with the remaining cheeses. Drizzle with the extra virgin olive oil.

Note: Ricotta salata is a lightly salted, pressed ricotta cheese. If unavailable, use a mild feta cheese.

OD RISOTTO

SERVE

2 ripe tomatoes

500 g (1 lb 2 oz) black mussels

315 ml (11 fl oz/1¼ cups) white wine

1.25 litres (44 fl oz/5 cups) fish stock

pinch of saffron threads

2 tablespoons olive oil

30 g (1 oz) butter

500 g (1 lb 2 oz) raw prawns (shrimp), peeled and deveined

225 g (8 oz) squid tubes, sliced into thin rings

200 g (7 oz) scallops

3 garlic cloves, crushed

1 onion, finely chopped

370 g (12 oz/2 cups) risotto rice (arborio, vialone nano or carnaroli)

2 tablespoons chopped parsley

1 Score a cross in the base of each tomato. Place in a bowl of boiling water for 10 seconds, then plunge into cold water and peel the skin away from the cross. Chop the tomato flesh.

2 Scrub the mussels with a stiff brush and remove the hairy beards. Discard any broken mussels or any that do not close when tapped. Pour the wine into a large saucepan and bring to the boil. Add the mussels and cook, covered, over medium heat for 3–5 minutes, or until the mussels open. Discard any that do not open. Strain, reserving the liquid. Remove the mussels from their shells.

3 Combine the mussel liquid, stock and saffron in a saucepan, cover and keep at a low simmer.

4 Heat the oil and butter in a large saucepan over medium heat. Add the prawns and cook until pink. Remove. Add the squid and scallops and cook for about 1–2 minutes, until white. Remove. Add the garlic and onion and cook for 3 minutes, or until golden. Add the rice and stir until coated.

5 Add 125 ml (4 fl oz/½ cup) of the hot liquid, stirring constantly until it is all absorbed. Continue adding liquid, 125 ml (4 fl oz/½ cup) at a time, stirring constantly, for about 25 minutes, or until the liquid is absorbed. Stir in the tomato, seafood and parsley and heat through. Season, to taste.

Note: You can use almost any combination of seafood for this risotto. Try small pieces of firm, white fish, clams or octopus.

MUSHROOM RISOTTO

SERVES 4–6

20 g (1 oz) dried porcini mushrooms (see Note)

1 litre (35 fl oz/4 cups) chicken or vegetable stock

2 tablespoons olive oil

100 g (4 oz) butter, chopped

650 g (1 lb 7 oz) small cap or Swiss brown mushrooms, stems trimmed, sliced

3 cloves garlic, crushed

80 ml (3 fl oz/⅓ cup) dry white vermouth

1 onion, finely chopped

440 g (14 oz/2 cups) risotto rice (arborio, vialone nano or carnaroli)

150 g (6 oz/1½ cups) grated parmesan cheese

1 Soak porcini mushrooms in 500 ml (17 fl oz/2 cups) warm water for 30 minutes. Drain, retaining the liquid, and chop.

2 Pour the liquid through a fine sieve lined with a paper towel. Combine with the stock in a saucepan and bring to the boil. Reduce the heat, cover and keep at a low simmer.

3 Heat half the oil and 40 g (1½ oz) of the butter in a large frying pan over high heat. Add all the mushrooms and the garlic to the pan and cook, stirring, for 10 minutes, or until soft and all the mushroom juices have been released. Reduce the heat to low and cook for another 5 minutes, or until all the juices have evaporated. Increase the heat, add the vermouth and cook for 2–3 minutes, until evaporated. Set aside.

4 Heat the remaining olive oil and 20 g (¾ oz) butter in a large saucepan over medium heat. Add the onion and cook for 10 minutes, or until soft. Add the rice and stir for 1–2 minutes,

or until well coated. Add 125 ml (4 fl oz/½ cup) stock to the pan and stir constantly over medium heat until all the liquid is absorbed. Continue adding more stock, 125 ml (4 fl oz/½ cup) at a time, stirring constantly for 20–25 minutes, or until tender and creamy.

5 Remove from the heat and stir in the mushrooms, parmesan cheese and the remaining butter. Season, to taste, with salt and freshly ground black pepper.

Note: Dried porcini mushrooms are available in small packets at the supermarket. Soak them for at least 30 minutes in warm water. Pass the soaking liquid through a fine sieve lined with a paper towel to ensure that all the grit is removed. If stored in a tightly sealed container, porcini mushrooms keep indefinitely.

CHICKEN CACCIATORA

SERVES 4

60 ml (2 fl oz/¼ cup) olive oil

1 large onion, finely chopped

3 garlic cloves, crushed

150 g (6 oz) pancetta, finely chopped

125 g (5 oz) button mushrooms, thickly
    sliced

1 large chicken (at least 1.6 kg/3 lb 8 oz),
    cut into 8 pieces

80 ml (3 fl oz/⅓ cup) dry vermouth or
    dry white wine

2 x 400 g (14 oz) tins chopped tomatoes

¼ teaspoon soft brown sugar

¼ teaspoon cayenne pepper

1 sprig of oregano

1 sprig of thyme

1 bay leaf

1 Heat half the olive oil in a large heatproof casserole dish. Add the onion and garlic and cook for 6–8 minutes over low heat, stirring, until the onion is golden. Add the pancetta and mushrooms, increase the heat and cook, stirring, for 4–5 minutes. Transfer to a bowl.

2 Add the remaining oil to the casserole dish and brown the chicken pieces, a few at a time, over medium heat. Season with salt and black pepper as they brown. Spoon off the excess fat and return all the chicken to the casserole dish. Increase the heat, add the vermouth to the dish and cook until the liquid has almost evaporated.

3 Add the chopped tomato, brown sugar, cayenne pepper, oregano, thyme and bay leaf, and stir in 80 ml (3 fl oz/⅓ cup) water to the dish. Bring to the boil, then stir in the reserved onion mixture. Reduce the heat, cover and simmer for 25 minutes, or until the chicken is tender but not falling off the bone.

4 If the liquid is too thin, remove the chicken from the casserole dish, increase the heat and boil until the liquid has thickened. Discard the sprigs of herbs and adjust the seasoning. Can be garnished with fresh oregano or thyme sprigs and served with steamed rice.

SERVES 4–6

60 ml (2 fl oz/¼ cup) olive oil
1 kg (2 lb 4 oz) spring lamb, cut into 2 cm (¾ inch) cubes
2 garlic cloves, crushed
6 sage leaves
1 sprig rosemary
1 tablespoon flour
125 ml (4 fl oz/½ cup) white wine vinegar
6 anchovy fillets

Excellent

1 **Heat the oil** in a heavy-based frying pan and cook the meat in batches over medium heat for 3–4 minutes, until browned on all sides.

2 **Return all the meat to the pan** and add the garlic, sage and rosemary. Season with salt and pepper, combine well and cook for 1 minute.

3 **Dust meat** with the flour using a fine sieve, then cook for another minute. Add vinegar; simmer for 30 seconds, then add 250 ml (9 fl oz/1 cup) water. Bring to a gentle simmer, lower the heat and cover, leaving the lid partially askew. Cook for 50–60 minutes, or until meat is tender, stirring occasionally and adding a little more water, if necessary.

4 **When the lamb is almost cooked,** mash the anchovies in a mortar and pestle with 1 tablespoon of the cooking liquid, until a paste is formed. Add to the lamb and cook, uncovered, for another 2 minutes. Delicious served with roast potatoes.

Notes: This dish is best served immediately but can be prepared in advance up to the end of Step 3. The anchovies should be added at the last moment or they overpower the delicate flavour of the lamb. The secret of success for this famous recipe depends very much on the quality of lamb used. Ideally, it should be just one month old and entirely milk-fed, but any spring lamb will still give tender results.

RILLED SQUID WITH SALSA VERDE

SERVES 6

1 kg (2 lb 4 oz) squid

250 ml (9 fl oz/1 cup) olive oil

2 tablespoons lemon juice

2 garlic cloves, crushed

2 tablespoons chopped oregano

2 tablespoons chopped flat-leaf (Italian) parsley, for serving

6 lemon wedges, for serving

SALSA VERDE

4 anchovy fillets, drained

1 tablespoon capers

1 garlic clove, crushed

7 g (¼ oz/¼ cup) chopped flat-leaf (Italian) parsley

7 g (¼ oz/¼ cup) basil

7 g (¼ oz/¼ cup) mint

2 teaspoons red wine vinegar

3 tablespoons extra virgin olive oil

1 teaspoon dijon mustard

1   To clean squid, hold onto the hood and gently pull the tentacles away from the head. Cut out the beak and discard with any intestines still attached to the tentacles. Rinse the tentacles in cold running water, then dry and cut into 5 cm (2 inch) lengths. Place them in a bowl. Clean out the hood cavity and remove the transparent quill. Under cold running water, pull away the skin, rinse and dry well. Cut into 1 cm (½ inch) rings and place in the bowl with the tentacles. Add the oil, lemon juice, garlic and oregano to the bowl, and toss to coat the squid. Leave to marinate for 30 minutes.

2   For the salsa verde, put the anchovies, capers garlic, parsley, basil and mint in a food processor and chop in short bursts until roughly blended. Transfer to a bowl and stir in the vinegar. Slowly mix in the oil, then the mustard. Season.

3   Heat a barbecue flatplate or grill until hot. Drain squid rings and cook them in batches for 1–2 minutes each side.

4   Sprinkle the squid rings with salt, pepper and the fresh parsley and serve with the salsa verde and lemon wedges.

CAPONATA WITH TUNA

SERVES 6

CAPONATA

500 g (1 lb 2 oz) ripe tomatoes

750 g (1 lb 10 oz) eggplant (aubergine),
  cut into 1 cm (½ inch) cubes

125 ml (4 fl oz/½ cup) olive oil

1 onion, chopped

3 celery stalks, chopped

2 tablespoons capers

125 g (5 oz/½ cup) green olives, pitted

1 tablespoon sugar

125 ml (4 fl oz/½ cup) red wine vinegar

6 x 200 g (7 oz) tuna steaks

olive oil, for brushing

1 Score a cross in the base of each tomato. Place the tomatoes into a bowl of boiling water for 20 seconds, then plunge them into cold water and peel the skin away from the cross. Cut the tomatoes into 1 cm (½ inch) cubes.

2 Sprinkle eggplant with salt and leave in a colander for 1 hour. Rinse under cold water and pat dry. Heat 2 tablespoons oil in a frying pan over a medium heat. Cook half the eggplant for 4–5 minutes, or until golden and soft. Remove from pan; drain on crumpled paper towels. Repeat with 2 tablespoons oil and the remaining eggplant.

3 Heat the remaining olive oil in the same pan, add the onion and celery, and cook for 5–6 minutes, or until softened. Reduce heat to low, add tomato and simmer for 15 minutes, stirring occasionally. Stir in the capers, olives, sugar and vinegar, season and continue to simmer, stirring occasionally, for 10 minutes, or until slightly reduced. Stir in the eggplant. Remove from the heat and cool to room temperature.

4 Heat a barbecue grill and brush lightly with olive oil. Cook the tuna for 2–3 minutes each side, or to your liking. Serve with the caponata.

PARMESAN AND ROSEMARY CRUSTED VEAL CHOPS

SERVES 4

4 veal chops

150 g (6 oz) fresh white breadcrumbs

75 g (3 oz) grated parmesan cheese

1 tablespoon rosemary, finely chopped

2 eggs, lightly beaten, seasoned

3 tablespoons olive oil

60 g (2 oz) butter

4 garlic cloves

1 **Trim the chops of excess fat** and sinew and flatten to 1 cm (½ inch) thickness. Pat the meat dry with paper towels. Combine the breadcrumbs, parmesan cheese and rosemary in a shallow bowl.

2 **Dip each chop in the beaten egg,** draining off the excess. Press both sides of the chops firmly in the crumbs.

3 **Heat the oil** and butter in a heavy-based frying pan over low heat, add the garlic and cook until golden. Discard the garlic.

4 **Increase heat to medium,** add the chops to the pan and cook for 4–5 minutes on each side, depending on the thickness of the chops, until golden and crisp. Transfer to a warm serving dish and season with salt and pepper.

PORK WITH SAGE AND CAPERS

SERVES 4

60 ml (2 fl oz/¼ cup) extra virgin olive oil

25 g (1 oz) unsalted butter

1 onion, finely chopped

100 g (4 oz) fresh white breadcrumbs

2 teaspoons chopped sage

1 tablespoon chopped flat-leaf parsley

2 teaspoons grated lemon zest

2½ tablespoons salted baby capers, rinsed and drained

1 egg

2 large pork fillets (about 500 g/1 lb 2 oz each)

8 large thin slices of streaky bacon or prosciutto

2 teaspoons plain (all-purpose) flour

100 ml (4 fl oz) dry vermouth

315 ml (10 fl oz/1¼ cups) chicken or vegetable stock

8 whole sage leaves, extra, to garnish

---

1 **Preheat oven** to 170°C (325°F/Gas 3). Heat 1 tablespoon of the oil and the butter in a frying pan, add the onion and cook for 5 minutes, or until lightly golden.

2 **Place the breadcrumbs,** chopped sage, parsley, lemon zest, ½ tablespoon capers and the cooked onion in a bowl. Add the egg and season well.

3 **Split each pork fillet** in half lengthways and open out. Spread the stuffing down the length of one and cover with the other fillet.

4 **Stretch the bacon** or prosciutto with the back of a knife and wrap each piece slightly overlapping around the pork to form a neat parcel. Tie with string at intervals.

5 **Place pork in a baking dish** and drizzle with 1 tablespoon of the oil. Bake for 1 hour. To test if the meat is cooked, insert a skewer in the thickest part. The juices should run clear. Remove the meat from the tin, cover with foil and leave to rest. Place the baking dish on the stovetop, add the flour and stir in well. Add vermouth and allow to bubble for 1 minute. Add the stock and stir while cooking to remove all the lumps. Simmer for 5 minutes. Add the remaining capers to the sauce.

6 **In a small saucepan,** heat remaining oil and when very hot, fry the whole sage leaves until crisp. Drain on crumpled paper towels.

7 **Slice the pork** into 1 cm (½ inch) slices. Spoon a little sauce over the pork and serve each portion with fried sage leaves on top.

BEEF PROVENÇALE

SERVES 6

1.5 kg (3 lb 5 oz) chuck steak, cut into 3 cm (1¼ inch) cubes

2 tablespoons olive oil

1 small onion, sliced

375 ml (13 fl oz/1½ cups) red wine

2 tablespoons chopped flat-leaf (Italian) parsley

1 tablespoon chopped rosemary

1 tablespoon chopped thyme

2 bay leaves

250 g (9 oz) speck, rind removed, cut into 1 x 2 cm (½ x ¾ inch) pieces

400 g (14 oz) tin crushed tomatoes

250 ml (9 fl oz/1 cup) beef stock

500 g (1 lb 2 oz) baby carrots

45 g (1½ oz/⅓ cup) pitted niçoise olives or other small black olive

1 **In a bowl,** combine the cubed beef with 1 tablespoon of the oil, the onion, 250 ml (9 fl oz/1 cup) of wine and half the herbs. Cover with plastic wrap and leave to marinate in the refrigerator overnight.

2 **Drain the beef,** reserving the marinade. Heat remaining oil in a large heavy-based saucepan and brown the beef and onion in batches. Remove from the pan.

3 **Add speck to the saucepan** and cook for 3–5 minutes, until crisp. Return the beef to the pan with the remaining wine and marinade and cook, scraping the residue from the base of the pan for 2 minutes, or until the wine has slightly reduced. Add the tomato and stock and bring the boil. Reduce the heat and add the remaining herbs. Season well, cover and simmer for 1½ hours.

4 **Add the carrots and olives** to the saucepan and cook, uncovered, for another 30 minutes, or until the meat and the carrots are tender. Before serving, check the seasoning and adjust, if necessary.

LAMB AND ARTICHOKE FRICASSÉE

SERVES 8

6 fresh globe artichokes (see Note)
60 ml (2 fl oz/¼ cup) lemon juice
2 large, ripe tomatoes
80 ml (3 fl oz/⅓ cup) olive oil
2 kg (4 lb 8 oz) diced lamb
750 g (1 lb 10 oz) brown onions, thinly sliced
1 tablespoon plain (all-purpose) flour
2 garlic cloves, crushed
185 ml (6 fl oz/¾ cup) white wine
350 ml (11 fl oz/1⅓ cups) chicken stock
1 bouquet garni
chopped flat-leaf (Italian) parsley, to garnish
lemon wedges, for serving

1 **To prepare the globe artichokes,** bring a large saucepan of water to the boil and add the lemon juice. Trim the stems from the artichokes and remove the tough outer leaves. Cut off the hard tips of the remaining leaves using scissors. Blanch the artichokes for 5 minutes. Remove and turn upside-down to drain. When cool enough to handle, use a small spoon to remove the choke from the centre of each. Scrape the bases well to remove all the membrane. Cut the artichokes into quarters and set aside.

2 **Score a cross in the base** of each tomato and place in a bowl of boiling water for 20 seconds. Plunge into cold water and peel away from the cross. Cut each tomato in half and scoop out the seeds with a teaspoon. Chop the tomatoes.

3 **Heat half the oil** in a deep heatproof casserole and fry batches of the lamb until golden. Add the remaining oil and cook the onion for about 8 minutes, until soft and caramelized. Add the flour and cook for 1 minute. Add the garlic, tomato, wine and chicken stock. Return the lamb to the pan add the bouquet garni and simmer, covered, for 1 hour.

4 **Place artichokes in the casserole** and simmer, uncovered, for another 15 minutes. Remove meat and artichokes with a slotted spoon and place in a serving dish. Keep warm. Discard the bouquet garni. Cook sauce over high heat until it thickens. Pour the sauce over the lamb and garnish with parsley. Serve with lemon wedges.

Note: If fresh artichokes are not available, use 270 g (10 oz/ 1 cup) marinated artichokes. Drain them well and then pat dry with paper towels.

MUSSELS IN TOMATO AND HERB SAUCE

SERVES 4

TOMATO AND HERB SAUCE

80 ml (3 fl oz/⅓ cup) olive oil

3 garlic cloves, finely chopped

¼ teaspoon dried chilli flakes

2 x 400 g (14 oz) tins tomatoes

pinch of caster (superfine) sugar, or to taste

8 slices crusty Italian bread

4 tablespoons olive oil

2 large garlic cloves, halved

1 kg (2 lb 4 oz) black mussels

1 red onion, finely chopped

6 sprigs of flat-leaf parsley

2 sprigs of thyme

2 sprigs of oregano

250 ml (9 fl oz/1 cup) white wine

chopped flat-leaf (Italian) parsley, extra, to garnish

thyme leaves, extra, to garnish

chopped oregano leaves, extra, to garnish

1 **Preheat oven** to 160°C (315°F/Gas 2–3). To make tomato and herb sauce, heat the oil in a saucepan, add the garlic and chilli flakes, and cook over low heat for 30 seconds without browning. Add the tomato, sugar and 80 ml (3 fl oz/⅓ cup) water. Season well and simmer, stirring often, for 15 minutes, or until the sauce has thickened and reduced.

2 **Lightly brush the bread** with olive oil using half the oil. Place the bread in a single layer on a baking tray and bake for 10 minutes, or until crisp and golden. While still warm, rub one side of each slice with garlic.

3 **Meanwhile**, scrub the mussels with a stiff brush and pull out the hairy beards. Discard any broken mussels or those that don't close when tapped on a bench. Rinse well.

4 **Heat the remaining olive oil** in a large saucepan. Add the onion. Cook for 3 minutes, or until softened but not browned.

Add the parsley, thyme, oregano sprigs and wine. Bring to the boil, then reduce the heat and simmer for 5 minutes.

5 **Add the mussels** and stir to coat in the onion and wine mixture. Cook, covered, over high heat for 3–4 minutes. Gently shake the pan often, to move the mussels around. Remove the mussels as they open. Discard any unopened mussels.

6 **Strain the wine mixture** into the tomato sauce, discarding the onion and herbs. Check the sauce and season if necessary. Add the mussels and toss well to coat in the mixture. Pile into a serving bowl and garnish with the extra parsley, thyme and oregano. Arrange the bread around the bowl and serve.

Note: You can keep mussels (uncleaned) for a day or two longer in a bucket of cold, salted water.

GREAT TASTES MEDITERRANEAN

OCTOPUS BRAISED IN TOMATO AND WINE

SERVES 6

500 g (1 lb 2 oz) ripe tomatoes

1 kg (2 lb 4 oz) baby octopus

60 ml (2 fl oz/¼ cup) olive oil

1 large brown onion, chopped

2 garlic cloves

350 ml (12 fl oz/1⅓ cups) dry white wine

¼ teaspoon saffron threads

2 sprigs thyme

2 tablespoons roughly chopped flat-leaf (Italian) parsley

1 **Score a cross in the base** of each tomato. Place tomatoes in a bowl of boiling water for 20 seconds, then plunge them into cold water. Peel the skin away from the cross. Cut each tomato in half and scoop out the seeds with a teaspoon. Chop the flesh.

2 **To clean each octopus,** use a small sharp knife and cut each head from the tentacles. Remove the eyes by cutting a round of flesh from the base of each head. To clean the heads, carefully slit them open and remove the gut. Rinse thoroughly. Cut the heads in half. Push out the beaks from the centre of the tentacles from the cut side. Cut the tentacles into sets of four or two, depending on the size of the octopus.

3 **Blanch all the octopus** in boiling water for 2 minutes then drain and allow to cool slightly. Pat dry with paper towels.

4 **Heat the olive oil** in heavy-based frying pan and cook the onion for 7–8 minutes over medium heat until lightly golden. Add the octopus and garlic to the pan and cook for another 2–3 minutes. Add tomato, wine, saffron and thyme. Add just enough water to cover the octopus.

5 **Simmer, covered, for 1 hour.** Uncover and cook for another 15 minutes, or until the octopus is tender and the sauce has thickened a little. The cooking time will vary quite a bit depending on the size of the octopus. Season, to taste. Serve hot or at room temperature, sprinkled with parsley.

GARLIC CHICKEN

SERVES 6

1 kg (2 lb 4 oz) boneless, skinless chicken thighs

1 tablespoon paprika

2 tablespoons olive oil

8 cloves garlic, unpeeled

60 ml (2 fl oz/¼ cup) brandy

125 ml (4 fl oz/½ cup) chicken stock

1 bay leaf

2 tablespoons chopped flat-leaf (Italian) parsley

1 Trim any excess fat from the chicken and cut the thighs into thirds. Combine the paprika with some salt and pepper in a bowl, add the chicken and toss to coat.

2 Heat half the oil in a large frying pan over high heat and cook the garlic for 1–2 minutes, until brown. Remove from the pan. Cook the chicken in batches for 5 minutes each batch, or until brown. Return all the chicken to the pan, add the brandy, boil for 30 seconds, then add the stock and bay leaf. Reduce the heat, cover and simmer over low heat for 10 minutes.

3 Meanwhile, place the garlic pulp in a mortar and pestle or small bowl. Add parsley and pound or mix with a fork to form a paste. Stir into the chicken, cover and cook for 10 minutes, or until tender. Serve hot.

PORK SAUSAGES WITH WHITE BEANS

SERVES 4

350 g (12 oz) dried white haricot beans

150 g (6 oz) speck or pancetta, in one piece

½ leek, thinly sliced

2 whole garlic cloves

1 bay leaf

1 small red chilli, split and seeds removed

1 small onion

2 cloves

1 sprig of rosemary

3 sprigs of thyme

1 sprig of parsley

3 tablespoons olive oil

8 pork sausages

1 small onion, finely chopped

1 green capsicum (pepper), finely chopped

½ teaspoon paprika

125 ml (4 fl oz/½ cup) tomato passata (puréed tomatoes)

1 teaspoon cider vinegar

1 Soak beans in plenty of cold water overnight. Drain and rinse the beans under cold water. Put them in a large saucepan with the tocino, leek, garlic, bay leaf and chilli. Stud the onion with the cloves and add to the saucepan. Tie the rosemary, thyme and parsley together and add to the saucepan. Pour in 750 ml (24 fl oz/3 cups) cold water and bring to the boil. Add 1 tablespoon oil, reduce the heat and simmer, covered, for about 1 hour, until the beans are tender. Add a little more boiling water when necessary, to keep the beans covered.

2 Prick each sausage 5 or 6 times and twist tightly in opposite directions in the middle to give 2 short fat sausages joined in the middle. Put in a single layer in a large frying pan and add enough cold water to reach halfway up their sides. Bring to the boil and simmer, turning two or three times, until

all the water has evaporated and the sausages brown lightly in the little fat that is left in the pan. Remove from the pan and cut the short sausages apart. Add the remaining 2 tablespoons oil, the chopped onion and green capsicum to the pan and fry over medium heat for 5–6 minutes. Stir in the paprika, cook for 30 seconds then add the puréed tomato. Season, to taste. Cook, stirring, for 1 minute.

3 Remove the tocino, herb sprigs and any loose large pieces of onion from the bean mixture. Leave in any loose leaves from the herbs, and any small pieces of onion. Add the sausages and sauce to the pan and stir the vinegar through. Bring to the boil. Adjust the seasoning.

Note: This dish improves if cooked in advance and left for up to 2 days before serving.

BAKED FISH WITH CAPSICUMS, CHILLI AND POTATOES

SERVES 4–6

1.25 kg (2 lb 14) whole red bream or red snapper, cleaned

1 lemon

3 tablespoons olive oil

800 g (1 lb 12 oz) potatoes, thinly sliced

3 garlic cloves, thinly sliced

3 tablespoons finely chopped parsley

1 small red onion, thinly sliced

1 small dried chilli, seeded and finely chopped, or a pinch of dried chilli flakes

1 red capsicum (pepper), cored, seeded and cut into thin rings

1 yellow capsicum (pepper), cored, seeded and cut into thin rings

2 bay leaves

3–4 sprigs of thyme

3 tablespoons dry sherry

1   Cut off and discard the fins from the fish and place it in a large non-metallic dish. Cut 2 thin slices from one end of the lemon and reserve. Squeeze the juice from the rest of the lemon inside the fish. Add 2 tablespoons oil. Refrigerate, covered, for 2 hours.

2   Preheat the oven to 190°C (375°F/Gas 5) and lightly oil a shallow earthenware baking dish large enough to hold the whole fish. Spread half the potatoes on the base and scatter the garlic, parsley, onion, chilli and capsicums on top. Season with salt and pepper. Cover with the remaining potatoes and pour in 80 ml (3 fl oz/⅓ cup) water. Sprinkle the remaining olive oil over the top. Cover with foil and bake for 1 hour.

3   Increase the oven temperature to 220°C (425°F/Gas 7). Season the fish inside and out with salt and pepper and place the bay leaves and thyme inside the cavity. Make 3–4 diagonal slashes on each side. Cut reserved lemon slices in half and fit these into the slashes on one side of the fish, to resemble fins. Nestle the fish into the potatoes with the lemon on top. Bake, uncovered, for 30 minutes, or until the fish is cooked through and the surrounding potatoes are golden and crusty.

4   Pour the dry sherry over the fish and return to the oven for 3 minutes. Serve straight from the dish.

ROAST CHICKEN STUFFED WITH PINE NUTS AND RICE

SERVES 4–6

STUFFING

60 g (2 oz) clarified butter (see Note)
  or ghee, melted

1 onion, chopped

1 teaspoon ground allspice

60 g (2 oz/⅓ cup) basmati rice

30 g (1 oz/¼ cup) walnuts, chopped

50 g (2 oz/⅓ cup) pine nuts

55 g (2 oz/⅓ cup) sultanas

125 ml (4 fl oz/½ cup) chicken stock

1.6 kg (3 lb 8 oz) chicken

½ teaspoon salt

¼ teaspoon cracked black pepper

170 ml (6 fl oz/⅔ fl oz) chicken stock

1 Preheat the oven to 180°C (350°F/Gas 4). Pour half the butter into a large frying pan, then add the onion. Cook for 5 minutes over medium heat until the onion is transparent. Stir in the allspice.

2 Add rice and nuts to the pan, then cook for 3–4 minutes over medium-high heat. Add the sultanas, stock and 60 ml (2 fl oz/¼ cup) of water. Bring to the boil, then reduce heat and simmer for 8–10 minutes, until the water is absorbed. Allow to cool.

3 Rinse the cavity of the chicken with cold water and pat dry inside and out with paper towels.

4 When the stuffing is cool, spoon it into the cavity. and truss the chicken, using string. Place in a deep baking dish and rub salt and black pepper into the skin using your fingertips.

5 Pour the rest of the butter over the chicken, then add stock to the pan. Roast for 2 hours 10 minutes, basting every 20–25 minutes with juices from the pan. Rest the chicken for 15 minutes before carving. Serve with the stuffing.

Note: To clarify butter, melt it in a saucepan over low heat, then remove from the heat and let the milk solids drop to the base. Only use the yellow liquid part of the butter. Discard the white milk solids at the base of the saucepan.

STUFFED LEG OF LAMB

SERVES 6–8

STUFFING

1 thick slice white country-style bread, crusts removed

70 g (2 oz) chicken livers, trimmed

60 g (2 oz) bacon

1 tablespoon dry sherry

1 garlic clove, crushed

1 tablespoon chopped flat-leaf parsley

½ tablespoon chopped chives

1 teaspoon finely chopped rosemary

1 tablespoon capers, finely chopped

1 large leg of lamb (about 3 kg/6 lb 10 oz), boned (see Note)

1 teaspoon sweet paprika (pimenton)

1 tablespoon plain (all-purpose) flour

¼ teaspoon salt

4 whole garlic cloves, peeled

2 tablespoons olive oil

375 ml (12 fl oz/1½ cups) dry white wine

1 tablespoon lard

125 ml (4 fl oz/½ cup) chicken or vegetable stock

1 **To make the stuffing,** break bread into pieces and process with the chicken livers and tocino until medium-fine. Place in a bowl with the sherry, garlic, parsley, chives, rosemary and capers. Season well with salt and freshly ground black pepper and mix well.

2 **Preheat oven** to 210°C (415°F/Gas 6–7). Lay the lamb out flat and place the filling down the centre. Roll the meat up to encase the filling. Tie up tightly with kitchen twine. Combine the paprika, flour and salt, and rub all over the surface of the lamb. Put the garlic in a row in the centre of a baking dish and pour the oil over the top. Place lamb on the garlic and pour the wine over the top. Spread the lard over the surface.

3 **Bake for 20 minutes,** then reduce the heat to 170°C (325°F/Gas 3). Baste, then bake for another 1 hour 45 minutes, basting frequently, until the lamb is well cooked. Transfer to a carving tray and keep warm. Spoon off excess oil from the pan juices then transfer the contents of the baking dish to a small saucepan; there will be about 125 ml (4 fl oz/½ cup). Add the stock and cook over high heat until slightly thickened. Taste for seasoning. Slice the lamb and arrange on a warm serving platter. Pour the sauce over the lamb and serve warm.

Note: Have your butcher bone the lamb and flatten out the meat to form a rough rectangle.

CHICKEN AND CHORIZO

SERVES 6

60 ml (2 fl oz/¼ cup) olive oil

1 large red capsicum (pepper), seeded and cut into 5 mm (¼ inch) strips

600 g (1 lb 5 oz) boneless, skinless chicken thighs, cut into 3 cm (1¼ inch) cubes

200 g (7 oz) chorizo sausage, cut into 2 cm (¾ inch) slices

200 g (7 oz) mushrooms, thinly sliced

3 garlic cloves, crushed

1 tablespoon grated lemon zest

700 g (1 lb 9 oz) ripe tomatoes, roughly chopped

200 g (7 oz) green beans, cut into 3 cm (1¼ inch) lengths

1 tablespoon chopped rosemary

2 tablespoons chopped flat-leaf (Italian) parsley

¼ teaspoon saffron threads dissolved in 60 ml (2 fl oz/¼ cup) hot water

440 g (16 oz/2 cups) short-grain rice

750 ml (27 fl oz/3 cups) hot chicken stock

6 lemon wedges, for serving

1 Heat the olive oil in a large, deep frying pan or paella pan over medium heat. Add the capsicum and cook for about 6 minutes, or until softened. Remove from the pan.

2 Add chicken to the pan and cook for 10 minutes, or until brown on all sides. Remove from pan. Add the sausage to the pan; cook for 5 minutes, or until golden on all sides. Remove from the pan. Add mushrooms, garlic and lemon zest to the pan; cook over medium heat for 5 minutes.

3 Stir in the tomato and capsicum, and cook for another 5 minutes, or until the tomato is soft.

4 Add the beans, rosemary, parsley, saffron mixture, rice, chicken and sausage. Stir briefly and add the stock. Do not stir at this point. Reduce the heat and simmer for 30 minutes. Remove from heat, cover and leave for 10 minutes. Serve with lemon wedges.

Note: Paella pans are available from specialist kitchenware shops. However, a large, heavy frying pan will work well.

MOROCCAN CHICKEN PIE

SERVES 6–8

200 g (7 oz) butter

1.5 kg (3 lb 5 oz) chicken, cut into 4 portions

1 large onion, finely chopped

3 teaspoons ground cinnamon

1 teaspoon ground ginger

2 teaspoons ground cumin

¼ teaspoon cayenne pepper

½ teaspoon ground turmeric

½ teaspoon saffron threads soaked in 2 tablespoons warm water

125 ml (4 fl oz/½ cup) chicken stock

4 eggs, lightly beaten

25 g (1 oz/½ cup) chopped coriander (cilantro) leaves

3 tablespoons chopped flat-leaf (Italian) parsley

50 g (2 oz/⅓ cup) chopped almonds

3 tablespoons icing (confectioners') sugar, plus extra, for dusting

375 g (13 oz) filo pastry

1 Preheat the oven to 180°C (350°F/Gas 4). Grease a 30 cm (12 inch) pizza tray.

2 Melt 40 g (1½ oz) of the butter in a large frying pan, add chicken, onion, 2 teaspoons of cinnamon, all the other spices and the chicken stock. Season with salt and pepper. Cover and simmer for 30 minutes, or until the chicken is cooked through.

3 Remove the chicken from the sauce. When cool enough to handle, remove the meat from the bones, discard the skin and bones and shred the meat into thin strips.

4 Bring the liquid in the pan to a simmer and add the eggs. Cook the mixture, stirring constantly, until the eggs are cooked and the mixture is quite dry. Add the chicken, chopped coriander and parsley, season well with salt and pepper and mix. Remove from the heat.

5 Bake the almonds on a baking tray until golden brown. Cool slightly, then blend in a food processor or spice grinder with the icing sugar and remaining cinnamon until they resemble coarse crumbs.

6 Melt remaining butter. Place a sheet of filo on the pizza tray and brush with melted butter. Place another sheet on top in a pinwheel effect and brush with butter. Continue brushing and layering until you have used 8 sheets. Place the chicken mixture on top and sprinkle with the almond mixture.

7 Fold the overlapping filo over the top of the filling. Place a sheet of filo over the top and brush with butter. Continue to layer buttered filo in the same pinwheel effect until you have used 8 sheets. Tuck the overhanging edges in to form a round parcel. Brush well with the remaining butter. Bake for about 45 minutes until golden. Dust with icing sugar before serving.

CYPRIOT PORK AND CORIANDER STEW

SERVES 4–6

1½ tablespoons coriander seeds

½ teaspoon cracked black pepper

800 g (1 lb 12 oz) pork fillet, cut into
  2 cm (¾ inch) dice

1 tablespoon plain (all-purpose) flour

60 ml (2 fl oz/¼ cup) olive oil

1 large onion, thinly sliced

375 ml (12 fl oz/1½ cups) red wine

250 ml (9 fl oz/1 cup) chicken stock

1 teaspoon sugar

fresh coriander (cilantro) sprigs,
  to garnish

1 **Crush coriander seeds** in a mortar and pestle. Transfer to a bowl, add cracked black pepper and pork and toss to coat. Cover and refrigerate overnight.

2 **Add the flour to the pork** and toss. Heat 2 tablespoons oil in a frying pan and cook the pork in batches over high heat for 1–2 minutes, or until brown. Remove from the pan.

3 **Heat the remaining oil** in the pan, add the onion and cook over medium heat for 2–3 minutes, or until just golden.

Return the meat to the pan, add the red wine, stock and sugar. Season, bring to the boil, then reduce the heat and simmer, covered, for 1 hour.

4 **Remove the meat.** Return the pan to the heat and boil over high heat for 3–5 minutes, or until the sauce is reduced and slightly thickened. Pour over the meat and garnish with coriander sprigs.

ROAST CHICKEN WITH ROSEMARY

SERVES 4

2 sprigs of rosemary

3 garlic cloves

1 teaspoon balsamic vinegar

1 x 1.5 kg (3 lb 5 oz) chicken

2 tablespoons extra virgin olive oil

2 tablespoons olive oil

125 ml (4 fl oz/½ cup) chicken stock

1 **Preheat oven** to 200°C (400°F/Gas 6). Put one rosemary sprig, the garlic and balsamic vinegar inside the cavity of the chicken. Add a large pinch of salt and a few grinds of black pepper. Truss the legs together.

2 **Rub the extra virgin olive oil** over chicken skin and pour the olive oil into a roasting tin. Put chicken in the tin, breast up. Place the second sprig of rosemary on top.

3 **Transfer to the oven** and roast for 1 hour, turning the chicken and basting with the pan juices every 15 minutes.

4 **Put chicken** on a warm serving plate and discard the rosemary sprig. Spoon off the fat from the roasting tin and place tin over high heat on the stovetop. Add the chicken stock and deglaze the pan. Boil until reduced and thickened. Taste for salt and pepper, then pour into a sauceboat to accompany the chicken.

VEAL SALTIMBOCCA

SERVES 4

8 small veal escalopes	
8 slices prosciutto	
8 sage leaves	
2 tablespoons olive oil	
60 g (2 oz) butter	
185 ml (6 fl oz/¾ cup) dry white wine or dry Marsala	

1 Place veal between two sheets of plastic wrap and pound with a meat mallet until an even thickness. Season lightly. Cut the prosciutto slices to the same size as the veal. Cover each piece of veal with a slice of prosciutto and place a sage leaf on top. Secure in place with a cocktail stick.

2 Heat oil and half the butter in a large frying pan. Add the veal in batches and fry, prosciutto up, over moderately high heat for 3–4 minutes, or until the veal is just cooked through. Transfer each batch to a warmed plate as it is done.

3 Pour off the oil from the pan and add the wine. Cook over high heat until reduced by half, scraping up the bits from the bottom of the pan. Add the remaining butter and, when it has melted, season. Spoon over the veal to serve.

OSSO BUCO WITH TOMATOES

SERVES 4

10 pieces veal shank, about 4 cm
(1½ inches) thick

plain (all-purpose) flour, seasoned with
salt and pepper

60 ml (2 fl oz/¼ cup) olive oil

60 g (2 oz) butter

1 garlic clove

1 small carrot, finely chopped

1 large onion, finely chopped

½ celery stalk, finely chopped

250 ml (9 fl oz/1 cup) dry white wine

375 ml (13 fl oz/1½ cups) veal or chicken
stock

400 g (14 oz) tin chopped tomatoes

bouquet garni

1 Tie each piece of veal shank around its girth to secure
the flesh, then dust with seasoned flour. Heat the oil, butter
and garlic in a large heavy saucepan big enough to hold the
shanks in a single layer. Put the shanks in the saucepan and
cook for 12–15 minutes until well browned. Remove the
shanks from the saucepan and set aside. Discard the garlic.

2 Add the carrot, onion and celery to the saucepan and
cook over moderate heat for 5–6 minutes, without browning.
Increase the heat to high, add the wine and cook for
2–3 minutes. Add the stock, tomatoes and bouquet garni.
Season with salt and pepper.

3 Return the veal shanks to the saucepan, standing them
up in a single layer. Cover the pan, reduce heat and simmer for
1 hour, or until the meat is tender and can be cut with a fork.

4 If you prefer a thicker sauce, remove the veal shanks and
increase the heat. Boil the sauce until reduced and thickened,
then return the veal to the saucepan. Discard bouquet garni,
and taste for salt and pepper.

ITALIAN MEATBALLS WITH TOMATO SAUCE

SERVES 4

1 onion, finely chopped

100 g (⅔ cup) pine nuts, roughly chopped

3 garlic cloves, crushed

40 g (1½ oz) parsley, roughly chopped

5 g (¼ oz) basil or rosemary, roughly chopped

2 teaspoons fennel seeds, ground

55 g (2 oz/⅔ cup) fresh breadcrumbs

250 g (9 fl oz/1 cup) ricotta cheese

25 g (1 oz/¼ cup) grated parmesan cheese

grated zest of 1 large lemon

1 egg

500 g (1 lb 2 oz) minced (ground) pork or beef

SAUCE

800 g (1 lb 12 oz) tomatoes or 2 x 400 g (14 oz) tins tomatoes

125 ml (4 fl oz/½ cup) red wine

1 Heat half the olive oil in a saucepan and cook the onion and pine nuts until onion is soft and pine nuts are light golden brown. Add the garlic and cook for a few minutes more, then set aside to cool.

2 Put herbs, fennel seeds, breadcrumbs, ricotta, parmesan cheese, lemon zest and egg in a bowl and add minced meat. Add the cooled onion and pine nuts, season with salt and pepper and mix briefly until all the ingredients are combined. Test for correct seasoning by frying one small meatball and tasting for flavour. Leave the mixture to rest in the fridge for at least 30 minutes or overnight.

3 To make the meatballs, roll a small amount of mixture into a ball about the size of a walnut and then flatten slightly to make it easier to cook on both sides. Repeat with the rest of the mixture.

4 Heat the remaining olive oil in a large saucepan and fry the meatballs until golden brown on both sides. If necessary, cook them in two batches to prevent the pan overcrowding. Make sure there is enough oil to prevent the meatballs sticking to the base of the saucepan. Remove all the meatballs from the pan.

5 To make the sauce, if you are using fresh tomatoes, score a cross in the top of each one, plunge them into boiling water for 20 seconds, then drain and peel the skin away from the cross. Finely chop the flesh. Add the tomatoes and wine to the saucepan, season with salt and pepper and simmer for 5 minutes. Gently add the meatballs to the sauce and reduce the heat to a gentle simmer. Cover the saucepan and cook for a further 10 minutes. Leave for 10 minutes before serving.

COQ AU VIN

SERVES 8

1 bottle red wine

2 bay leaves

2 thyme sprigs

250 g (9 oz/1¾ cup) bacon, diced

60 g (2 oz) butter

20 baby or pearl onions

250 g (9 oz/2½ cups) button
   mushrooms

1 teaspoon oil

30 g (1 oz) plain (all-purpose) flour

1 litre (35 fl oz/4 cups) chicken stock

125 ml (4 fl oz/½ cup) brandy

2 teaspoons tomato purée

1½ tablespoons softened butter

1 tablespoon plain (all-purpose) flour

2 tablespoons chopped parsley

1 **Joint each chicken** into eight pieces by removing both legs and cutting between the joint of the drumstick and the thigh. Cut down either side of the backbone and lift it out. Turn the chicken over and cut through the cartilage down the centre of the breastbone. Cut each breast in half, leaving the wing attached to the top half.

2 **Put the wine,** bay leaves, thyme and some salt and pepper in a bowl and add the chicken. Cover and leave to marinate, preferably overnight.

3 **Blanch the bacon** in boiling water, then drain, pat dry and sauté in a frying pan until golden. Lift out onto a plate. Melt a quarter of the butter in the pan, add the onions and sauté until browned. Lift out and set aside.

4 **Melt another quarter of the butter,** add the mushrooms, season with salt and pepper and sauté for 5 minutes. Remove.

5 **Drain the chicken,** reserving the marinade, and pat the chicken dry. Season. Add the remaining butter and the oil to the frying pan, add the chicken and sauté until golden. Stir in the flour.

6 **Transfer the chicken** to a large saucepan or casserole and add the stock. Pour the brandy into the frying pan and boil, stirring, for 30 seconds to deglaze the pan. Pour over the chicken. Add the marinade, onions, mushrooms, bacon and tomato purée. Cook over moderate heat for 45 minutes, or until the chicken is cooked through.

7 **If the sauce needs thickening,** lift out the chicken and vegetables and bring the sauce to the boil. Mix together the butter and flour to make a beurre manié and whisk into the sauce. Boil, stirring, for 2 minutes until thickened. Add the parsley and return the chicken and vegetables to the sauce.

CHICKEN CHASSEUR

SERVES 4

1 x 1.6 kg (3 lb 8 oz) chicken
1 tablespoon oil
60 g (2 oz) butter
2 French shallots, finely chopped
125 g (5 oz) button mushrooms, sliced
1 tablespoon plain (all-purpose) flour
125 ml (4 fl oz/½ cup) white wine
2 tablespoons brandy
2 teaspoons tomato paste (concentrated purée)
250 ml (9 fl oz/1 cup) chicken stock
2 teaspoons chopped tarragon
1 teaspoon chopped parsley

CROUTONS

2 slices bread
olive oil

1 **Joint the chicken** into eight pieces by removing both legs and cutting between the joint of the drumstick and the thigh. Cut down either side of the backbone and lift it out. Turn the chicken over and cut through the cartilage down the centre of the breastbone. Cut each breast in half, leaving the wing attached to the top half.

2 **Heat the oil** in a frying pan or saucepan and add half the butter. When the foaming subsides, add the chicken and sauté in batches on both sides until browned. Lift out onto a plate and keep warm. Pour the excess fat out of the pan.

3 **Melt remaining butter** in the pan, add shallots and cook gently until softened but not browned. Add the mushrooms and cook, covered, over moderate heat for 3 minutes.

4 **Add the flour** and cook, stirring constantly, for 1 minute. Stir in the white wine, brandy, tomato paste and stock. Bring to the boil, stirring constantly, then reduce the heat and add the tarragon. Season.

5 **Return the chicken** to the pan, cover and simmer for 30 minutes, or until the chicken is tender and cooked through. Sprinkle with parsley to serve.

6 **To make croutons,** trim the crusts from the bread and cut the bread into moon shapes with a biscuit cutter. Heat the olive oil in a frying pan and fry bread until golden. Drain the croutons on paper towels and serve hot with the chicken.

TARRAGON CHICKEN

SERVES 4

1½ tablespoons chopped tarragon

1 small garlic clove, crushed

50 g (2 oz) butter, softened

1 x 1.6 kg (3 lb 8 oz) chicken

2 teaspoons oil

170 ml (6 fl oz/⅔ cup) chicken stock

2 tablespoons white wine

1 tablespoon plain (all-purpose) flour

1 tablespoon tarragon

170 ml (6 fl oz/⅔ cup) thick (double/ heavy) cream

1 **Preheat the oven** to 200°C (400°F/Gas 6). Combine the chopped tarragon, garlic and half the butter. Season with salt and pepper and place inside the cavity of the chicken. Tie the legs together and tuck the wing tips under.

2 **Heat remaining butter** with the oil in a large casserole dish over low heat and brown chicken on all sides. Add the chicken stock and wine. Cover the casserole and bake in the oven for 1 hour 20 minutes, or until chicken is tender and the juices run clear when the thigh is pierced with a skewer. Remove chicken, draining all the juices back into the casserole. Cover with baking foil and a tea towel (dish towel) and leave the chicken to rest.

3 **Skim a tablespoon of the surface fat** from the cooking liquid and put it in a small bowl. Skim the remainder of the fat from the surface and throw this away. Add the flour to the reserved fat and mix until smooth. Whisk quickly into the cooking liquid and stir over moderate heat until the sauce boils and thickens.

4 **Strain sauce** into a clean saucepan and add the tarragon leaves. Simmer for 2 minutes, then stir in the cream; reheat without boiling. Season with salt and pepper. Carve chicken and spoon the sauce over the top to serve.

BEEF CARBONNADE

SERVES 4

30 g (1 oz) butter

2–3 tablespoons oil

1 kg (2 lb 4 oz) lean beef rump or chuck
   steak, cubed

4 onions, chopped

1 garlic clove, crushed

1 teaspoon brown sugar

1 tablespoon plain (all-purpose) flour

500 ml (17 fl oz/2 cups) beer (bitter or
   stout)

2 bay leaves

4 sprigs of thyme

CROUTONS

6–8 slices baguette

dijon mustard

1   Preheat the oven to 150°C (300°F/Gas 2). Melt the butter in a large sauté pan with a tablespoon of oil. Brown the meat in batches over high heat and then lift out onto a plate.

2   Add another tablespoon of oil to the pan and add the onion. Cook over a moderate heat for 10 minutes, then add the garlic and sugar and cook for a further 5 minutes, adding another tablespoon of oil if necessary. Lift out the onion onto a second plate.

3   Reduce the heat to low and pour in any juices that have drained from the browned meat. Stir in the flour. Remove from the heat and stir in the beer, a little at a time (it will foam as it goes in). Return to the heat and let the mixture gently simmer and thicken. Season with salt and pepper.

4   Layer the meat and onion in a casserole dish, tucking the bay leaves and sprigs of thyme between the layers and seasoning with salt and black pepper as you go. Pour the liquid over the meat, cover with a lid and cook in the oven for 2½–3 hours, or until the meat is tender.

5   To make the croutons, preheat the grill (broiler). Lightly toast the baguette on both sides, then spread one side with mustard. Arrange on top of the carbonnade, mustard side up, and place the whole casserole under the grill for a minute.

PORK CHOPS WITH BRAISED RED CABBAGE

SERVES 4

30 g (1 oz) clarified butter

1 onion, finely chopped

1 garlic clove, crushed

1 small red cabbage, shredded

1 dessert apple, peeled and sliced

80 ml (3 fl oz/⅓ cup) red wine

1 tablespoon red wine vinegar

¼ teaspoon ground cloves

1 tablespoon finely chopped sage

1 tablespoon clarified butter

4 x 200 g (7 oz) pork chops, trimmed

80 ml (3 fl oz/⅓ cup) white wine

410 ml (14 fl oz/1¾ cups) chicken stock

3 tablespoons thick (double/heavy) cream

1½ tablespoons dijon mustard

4 sage leaves

1 To braise cabbage, put the clarified butter in a large saucepan, add the onion and garlic and cook until softened but not browned. Add the cabbage, apple, wine, vinegar, cloves and sage and season with salt and pepper. Cover pan and cook for 30 minutes over very low heat. Uncover pan and cook, stirring, for a further 5 minutes to evaporate any liquid.

2 Meanwhile, heat the clarified butter in a frying pan, season the chops and brown well on both sides. Add wine and stock, cover and simmer for 20 minutes, or until the pork is tender.

3 Remove the chops from the frying pan and strain the liquid. Return the liquid to the pan, bring to the boil and cook until reduced by two-thirds. Add the cream and mustard and stir over very low heat without allowing to boil, until the sauce has thickened slightly. Pour over the pork chops and garnish with sage. Serve with the red cabbage.

ROAST LEG OF LAMB WITH SPRING VEGETABLES

SERVES 6

1 x 2 kg (4 lb 8 oz) leg of lamb
3 sprigs of rosemary
6 garlic cloves, unpeeled
500 g (1 lb 2 oz) small potatoes, halved
250 g (9 oz) baby carrots
6 small leeks
250 g (9 oz) small zucchini (courgettes)
1½ tablespoons plain (all-purpose) flour
125 ml (4 oz/½ cup) red wine
170 ml (6 fl oz/⅔ cup) brown stock

1 Preheat the oven to 200°C (400°F/Gas 6). Rub the lamb all over with salt and pepper. Put the lamb in a roasting tin, lay the sprigs of rosemary on top and scatter the garlic around the lamb. Roast for 20 minutes, then turn the lamb over.

2 Add the potatoes to the roasting tin and toss in the lamb fat, then return to the oven for a further 15 minutes. Turn the lamb again and cook for another 15 minutes.

3 Add the baby carrots and leeks to the tin, toss with the potatoes in the lamb fat and turn the lamb again. Roast for 15 more minutes, then add zucchini. Toss all the vegetables in the lamb fat and turn the leg of lamb again.

4 Roast for another 15 minutes, then lift the lamb out of the roasting tin to rest. The lamb will be rare—if you prefer, cook it for another 5–10 minutes. Remove the vegetables and garlic from the tin and keep warm.

5 To make the gravy, spoon the fat from the surface of the meat juices. Place the roasting tin over moderate heat on the stovetop and stir in the flour to make a roux. Cook, stirring, for 2 minutes, then gradually stir in the wine and stock. Boil the gravy for 2 minutes, then strain into a serving jug.

6 Carve the lamb and serve with the spring vegetables and garlic. Serve the gravy separately.

PAN-FRIED CALAMARI

SERVES 4

500 g (1 lb 2 oz) small squid

¼ teaspoon salt

2 tablespoons olive oil

PICADA

2 tablespoons extra virgin olive oil

2 tablespoons finely chopped flat-leaf
(Italian) parsley

1 garlic clove, crushed

¼ teaspoon ground black pepper

1   **To clean the squid**, gently pull the tentacles away from the tube (the intestines should come away at the same time). Remove the intestines from the tentacles by cutting under the eyes, then remove the beak if it remains in the centre of the tentacles by using your fingers to push up the centre. Pull away the soft bone from the hood.

2   **Rub the tubes** under cold running water. The skin should come away easily. Wash the hoods and tentacles and drain well. Transfer to a bowl, add the salt and mix well. Cover and refrigerate for 30 minutes.

3   **Close to serving time**, whisk the picada ingredients with some salt in a bowl.

4   **Heat the oil** in a frying pan over high heat and cook the squid hoods in small batches for 2–3 minutes, or until the hoods turn white and are tender. Cook the squid tentacles, turning to brown them all over, for 1 minute, or until they curl up. Serve hot, drizzled with the picada.

SERVES 4

4 x 200 g (7 oz) tuna steaks

80 ml (3 fl oz/⅓ cup) lemon juice

2 tablespoons chopped flat-leaf (Italian) parsley

170 ml (6 fl oz/⅔ cup) olive oil

1 brown onion, finely chopped

2 garlic cloves, chopped

400 g (14 oz) tin chopped tomatoes

1 bay leaf

1 teaspoon caster (superfine) sugar

1 teaspoon chopped thyme

plain (all-purpose) flour, for dusting

1 **Combine the tuna steaks** with the lemon juice, half the parsley and a large pinch of salt, and leave to marinate for 15 minutes. Preheat the oven to 180°C (350°F/gas 4).

2 **Heat 80 ml (3 fl oz/⅓ cup)** of the oil in a saucepan over medium heat and cook the onion and garlic for 5 minutes, or until softened. Add the tomato, bay leaf, sugar, thyme and remaining parsley, and season to taste. Increase heat to high and cook 3 minutes, or until some of the liquid has reduced.

3 **Heat remaining oil** in a large frying pan over medium–high heat. Drain the tuna steaks and coat in the flour. Cook for about 3 minutes each side, or until golden, then transfer to a casserole dish. Cover with the tomato sauce and bake for about 15 minutes, or until the tuna flakes easily.

WITH PRESERVED LEMON AND OLIVES

¼ preserved lemon (in jars from supermarkets and delicatessens)

3 tablespoons olive oil

1.6 kg (3 lb 8 oz) chicken

1 brown onion, chopped

2 garlic cloves, chopped

625 ml (22 fl oz/2½ cups) chicken stock

½ teaspoon ground ginger

1½ teaspoons ground cinnamon

pinch of saffron threads

100 g (4 oz/½ cup) green olives

2 bay leaves

2 chicken livers

3 tablespoons chopped coriander (cilantro) leaves

1 Rinse preserved lemon quarter under cold running water, remove and discard pulp and membranes. Drain rind, pat dry with paper towel and cut into strips. Set aside.

2 Preheat oven to 180°C (350°F/Gas 4). Heat 2 tablespoons of the olive oil in a large frying pan, add chicken and brown on all sides. Place in a deep baking dish.

3 Heat remaining oil in pan over medium heat, add onion and garlic and cook for 5 minutes, or until onion has softened. Add the chicken stock, ginger, cinnamon, saffron, olives, bay leaves and preserved lemon strips. Stir well, then pour sauce around the chicken in the dish. Bake for 1½ hours, or until

cooked through, adding a little more water or stock if sauce gets too dry. Baste the chicken during cooking.

4 Remove chicken from the dish, cover with foil and leave to rest. Pour the contents of the baking dish into a frying pan and place over a medium heat. Add chicken livers and mash them into the sauce as they cook. Cook for 5–6 minutes, or until the sauce has reduced and thickened. Add the chopped coriander. Cut chicken into pieces and serve with the sauce.

SLOW-ROASTED LAMB WITH

SERVES 6

2.25 kg (5 lb) leg of lamb

70 g (2 oz) butter, softened at room temperature

3 garlic cloves, crushed

2 teaspoons ground cumin

3 teaspoons ground coriander

1 teaspoon paprika

¼ teaspoon salt

1 tablespoon ground cumin, extra, to serve

1½ teaspoons coarse salt, extra, to serve

1 **Preheat oven** to 220°C (425°F/Gas 7). With a small sharp knife, cut small deep slits in the top and sides of the lamb.

2 **Mix the butter,** garlic, spices and salt in a bowl to form a smooth paste. With the back of a spoon, rub the paste all over the lamb, then use your fingers to spread the paste evenly, making sure all the lamb is covered.

3 **Put lamb, bone side down,** in a deep roasting tin and place on the top shelf of the oven. Bake for 10 minutes, then baste with the pan juices and return it to the centre shelf of the oven. Reduce oven temperature to 160°C (315°F/Gas 2–3). Bake for 3¼ hours, basting every 20–30 minutes, to ensure the lamb stays tender and flavoursome. Carve the lamb into chunky pieces. Mix the extra cumin with the coarse salt and serve on the side for sprinkling over.

SALADS & SIDES

LENTIL SALAD

SERVES 4–6

1 small onion

2 cloves

300 g (11 oz/1½ cups) puy lentils (see Note)

1 strip lemon zest

2 garlic cloves, peeled

1 bay leaf

2 teaspoons ground cumin

2 tablespoons red wine vinegar

60 ml (2 fl oz/¼ cup) olive oil

1 tablespoon lemon juice

2 tablespoons finely chopped mint

3 spring onions (scallions), finely chopped

1 Stud the onion with the cloves and place in a saucepan with the lentils, rind, garlic, bay leaf, 1 teaspoon cumin and 875 ml (31 fl oz/3½ cups) water. Bring to the boil and simmer gently over medium heat for 25–30 minutes, or until the lentils are tender. Drain off any excess liquid and discard the onion, rind and bay leaf. Reserve the garlic and finely chop.

2 Whisk together the vinegar, oil, juice, garlic and the remaining cumin. Stir the dressing through the lentils with the mint and spring onion. Season well, then leave for 30 minutes to allow the flavours to develop. Serve at room temperature.

Note: Puy lentils are small green lentils, available from gourmet food stores.

GREEK SALAD

1 telegraph (long) cucumber, peeled

2 green capsicums (peppers)

4 vine-ripened tomatoes, cut into wedges

1 red onion, finely sliced

16 kalamata olives

250 g (9 oz) Greek feta cheese, cubed

24 flat-leaf (Italian) parsley leaves

12 whole mint leaves

125 ml (4 fl oz/½ cup) good-quality olive oil

2 tablespoons lemon juice

1 garlic clove, crushed

1   Cut cucumber in half lengthways and discard the seeds. Cut into bite-sized pieces. Cut each pepper in half lengthways, remove the membrane and seeds and cut the flesh into 1 cm (½ inch) wide strips. Gently mix the cucumber, green pepper, tomato, onion, olives, feta cheese, parsley and mint in a large salad bowl.

2   Place the oil, lemon juice and garlic in a screw top jar, season and shake well. Pour over the salad and serve.

HALOUMI WITH SALAD AND GARLIC BREAD

SERVES 4

4 firm, ripe tomatoes

1 Lebanese (short) cucumber

140 g (5 oz) rocket (arugula)

80 g (3 oz/½ cup) kalamata olives

1 loaf crusty unsliced white bread

5 tablespoons olive oil

1 large garlic clove, cut in half

400 g (14 oz) haloumi cheese

1 tablespoon lemon juice

1 tablespoon chopped oregano

1 **Preheat the oven** to 180°C (350°F/Gas 4). Heat the grill (broiler) to high.

2 **Cut the tomatoes and cucumber** into bite-sized chunks and place in a serving dish with the rocket and olives. Mix well.

3 **Slice the bread** into eight 1.5 cm (½ inch) slices, drizzle 1½ tablespoons of the olive oil over the bread and season with salt and pepper. Grill (broil) until lightly golden, then rub each slice thoroughly with a cut side of the garlic. Wrap loosely in foil and keep warm in the oven.

4 **Cut the haloumi** into 8 slices. Heat ½ tablespoon of the oil in a shallow frying pan and fry the haloumi slices for 1–2 minutes on each side, until crisp and golden brown.

5 **Whisk together the lemon juice**, oregano and remaining olive oil to use as a dressing. Season, to taste. Pour half the dressing over the salad and toss well. Arrange the haloumi on top and drizzle with dressing. Serve immediately with the warm garlic bread.

GREEN OLIVE, WALNUT AND POMEGRANATE SALAD

SERVES 4

100 g (4 oz/1 cup) walnut halves
125 ml (4 fl oz/½ cup) olive oil
1½ tablespoons pomegranate syrup
½ teaspoon chilli flakes
350 g (12 oz/2 cups) green olives, pitted and cut in halves
175 g (6 oz/1 cup) pomegranate seeds
1 large red onion, chopped
2 large handfuls flat-leaf (Italian) parsley leaves

1 Soak walnut halves in boiling water for 3–4 minutes, or until the skins peel off readily. Drain, peel and pat dry. Lightly toast under a medium grill and when cool, roughly chop.

2 Combine olive oil, pomegranate syrup and chilli flakes in a screw-top jar and shake well.

3 Place the olives, pomegranate seeds, onion, walnuts and parsley in a bowl and toss. Just before serving, pour the dressing over, season, to taste, and combine well.

INSALATA CAPRESE

SERVES 4

3 large vine-ripened tomatoes

250 g (9 oz) bocconcini

12 basil leaves

60 ml (2 fl oz/¼ cup) extra virgin olive oil

4 basil leaves, roughly torn, extra

1 **Slice the tomato** into twelve 1 cm (½ inch) slices. Slice the bocconcini into 24 slices the same thickness as the tomato.

2 **Arrange the tomato slices** on a serving plate, alternating them with 2 slices of bocconcini and placing a basil leaf between the bocconcini slices.

3 **Drizzle with the olive oil**, sprinkle with the torn basil and season well with salt and freshly ground black pepper.

Note: You could use whole cherry tomatoes and toss them with the bocconcini and basil.

TUNA AND CANNELLINI BEAN SALAD

SERVES 4–6

400 g (14 oz) tuna steaks

1 tablespoon olive oil

1 small red onion, thinly sliced

1 ripe tomato, seeded and chopped

1 small red capsicum (pepper), thinly sliced

2 x 400 g (14 oz) tins cannellini beans

2 garlic cloves, crushed

1 teaspoon chopped thyme

4 tablespoons chopped flat-leaf (Italian) parsley

1½ tablespoons lemon juice

80 ml (3 fl oz/⅓ cup) extra virgin olive oil

1 teaspoon honey

100 g (4 oz) rocket (arugula)

1 teaspoon lemon zest

1 Heat the grill or barbecue. Place tuna steaks on a plate, brush with the oil and sprinkle with cracked black pepper on both sides. Cover with plastic wrap; refrigerate until needed.

2 Combine the onion, tomato and red capsicum in a large bowl. Rinse the cannellini beans under cold running water for 30 seconds, drain and add to the bowl with the garlic, thyme and 3 tablespoons of the parsley.

3 Place the lemon juice, oil and honey in a small saucepan, bring to the boil, then reduce the heat to low and simmer, stirring, for 1 minute, or until the honey dissolves. Remove from the heat.

4 Sear the tuna for 1 minute on each side. The meat should still be pink in the middle. Slice into 3 cm (1 inch) cubes and combine with the salad. Pour on the warm dressing and toss well.

5 Place the rocket on a large platter. Top with the salad, season and garnish with the lemon zest and remaining parsley. Serve immediately.

Note: Good-quality tinned tuna is a delicious substitute for the fresh tuna in this recipe. Drain well before using.

PIQUANT POTATO SALAD

SERVES 4

500 g (1 lb 2 oz) new potatoes

2 teaspoons chopped dill

2 spring onions (scallions), chopped

1 tablespoon capers, coarsely chopped

2 tablespoons extra virgin olive oil

1½ tablespoons lemon juice

1 teaspoon finely grated orange zest

1 Place the potatoes in a large saucepan of salted water and bring to the boil. Cook for 10 minutes, or until tender when pierced with a knife. Drain well.

2 Place the potatoes in a bowl with the dill, onion, capers and some salt and pepper. Mix well to combine. Whisk together the oil, lemon juice and orange rind in a small bowl and pour over the hot potatoes. Mix together and serve warm.

Note: Any small, waxy potato works well in this delicious salad. You can choose from those which are readily available such as pink fir, bintje or kipfler.

RUSSIAN SALAD

SERVES 4–6

MAYONNAISE
2 egg yolks

1 teaspoon dijon mustard

¼ teaspoon salt

125 ml (4 fl oz/½ cup) extra virgin olive oil

2 tablespoons lemon juice

2 small garlic cloves, crushed

---

3 tinned artichoke hearts (about 120 g/4 oz)

3 waxy potatoes (such as desiree), unpeeled

100 g (4 oz) baby green beans, trimmed and cut into 1 cm (½ inch) lengths

1 large carrot, cut into 1 cm (½ inch) dice

125 g (5 oz) fresh peas

30 g (1 oz) cornichons, chopped

2 tablespoons baby capers, rinsed

10 black olives cut into 3 slices

4 anchovy fillets, finely chopped

5 whole black olives, to garnish

---

1 **For the mayonnaise,** using electric beaters, beat egg yolks with the mustard and salt until creamy. Gradually add oil in a fine stream, beating constantly until all the oil has been added. Add the lemon juice, garlic and 1 teaspoon boiling water and beat for 1 minute until well combined. Season, to taste.

2 **Cut each artichoke into quarters.** Rinse potatoes, cover them with cold, salted water and bring to a gentle simmer. Cook for 15–20 minutes, or until tender when pierced with a knife. Drain; allow to cool slightly, then peel and set aside. When completely cool, cut into 1 cm (½ inch) dice.

3 **Blanch the beans** in boiling salted water until tender but still firm to the bite. Refresh in cold water; drain thoroughly. Repeat with the carrot and peas.

4 **Set aside a small quantity** of each vegetable, including the cornichons, for the garnish and season, to taste. Place the remainder in a bowl with the capers, anchovies and sliced olives. Add the mayonnaise, toss to combine and season, to taste. Arrange on a serving dish and garnish with the reserved vegetables and the whole olives.

Note: This Russian salad can be prepared up to 2 days in advance and stored in the refrigerator but should be served at room temperature.

PANZANELLA

SERVES 6–8

1 small red onion, sliced into thin rings

250 g (9 oz) stale bread such as ciabatta, crusts removed

4 ripe tomatoes

6 anchovy fillets, finely chopped

1 small garlic clove, crushed

1 tablespoon baby capers, chopped

2 tablespoons red wine vinegar

125 ml (4 fl oz/½ cup) extra virgin olive oil

2 small Lebanese (short) cucumbers, peeled and sliced

30 g (1 oz/1 cup) basil leaves, torn

1 In a small bowl, cover the onion with cold water and leave for 5 minutes. Squeeze the rings in your hand, closing tightly and letting go and repeating that process about five times. This removes the acid from the onion. Repeat the whole process twice more, using fresh water each time.

2 Tear the bread into rough 3 cm (1 inch) squares and toast lightly under a grill (broiler) for 4 minutes, or until bread is crisp but not browned. Allow to cool. Set aside.

3 Score a cross in the base of each tomato and place in boiling water for 20 seconds. Plunge them into cold water and peel away from the cross. Cut each tomato in half and scoop out seeds with a teaspoon. Roughly chop two of the tomatoes and purée the other two.

4 Combine the anchovies, garlic and capers in a screw-top jar. Add vinegar and olive oil, screw the lid on tightly and shake well. Season, then transfer to a large bowl and add the bread, onion, puréed and chopped tomato, cucumber and basil. Toss well and season, to taste. Leave to stand for at least 15 minutes to allow the flavours to develop. Serve at room temperature.

SALAD NIÇOISE

SERVES 4

3 eggs

2 vine-ripened tomatoes

175 g (6 oz) baby green beans, trimmed

125 ml (4 fl oz/½ cup) olive oil

2 tablespoons white wine vinegar

1 large garlic clove, halved

325 g (11 oz) iceberg lettuce heart, cut into 8 wedges

1 small red capsicum (pepper), seeded and sliced thinly

1 Lebanese (short) cucumber, cut into thin 5 cm (2 inch) lengths

1 celery stalk, cut into thin 5 cm (2 inch) lengths

¼ large red onion, thinly sliced

2 x 185 g (7 oz) tins tuna, drained, broken into chunks

12 kalamata olives

45 g (1½ oz) tin anchovy fillets, drained

2 teaspoons baby capers

12 small basil leaves

1 **Place eggs** in a saucepan of cold water. Bring to the boil, then reduce the heat and simmer for 10 minutes. Stir during the first couple of minutes to centre the yolks. Cool under cold water; peel and cut into quarters. Meanwhile, score a cross in the base of each tomato and place in a bowl of boiling water for 10 seconds. Plunge into cold water and peel away from the cross. Cut each tomato into eight.

2 **Cook beans** in a saucepan of boiling water for 2 minutes, rinse under cold water, then drain.

3 **For the dressing,** place the oil and vinegar in a jar and shake to combine.

4 **Rub the garlic** over base and sides of a platter. Arrange the lettuce over the base. Layer the egg, tomato, beans, red pepper, cucumber and celery over the lettuce. Scatter the onion and tuna over them, then the olives, anchovies, capers and basil. Drizzle with dressing and serve.

ROASTED FENNEL AND ORANGE SALAD

SERVES 4

8 baby fennel bulbs

5 tablespoons olive oil

2 oranges

1 tablespoon lemon juice

1 red onion, halved and thinly sliced

100 g (4 oz) kalamata olives

2 tablespoons roughly chopped mint

1 tablespoon roughly chopped flat-leaf
(Italian) parsley

1   **Preheat the oven** to 200°C (400°F/Gas 6). Trim the fronds from the fennel and reserve. Remove stalks and cut a slice off the base of each fennel about 5 mm (¼ inch) thick. Slice each fennel into 6 wedges, place in a baking dish and drizzle with 3 tablespoons olive oil. Season well. Bake for 40–45 minutes, or until the fennel is tender and slightly caramelized. Turn once or twice during cooking. Allow to cool.

2   **Cut a thin slice** off the top and bottom of each orange. Using a small sharp knife, slice skin and pith off the oranges. Remove as much pith as possible. Slice down the side of a segment between the flesh and the membrane. Repeat with the other side and lift the segment out. Do this over a bowl to catch the juices. Repeat with all the segments on both. Squeeze out any juice remaining in the membranes.

3   **Whisk the remaining oil** into the orange juice and the lemon juice until emulsified. Season well. Combine the orange segments, onion and olives in a bowl, pour on half the dressing and add half the mint. Mix well. Transfer to a serving dish. Top with the roasted fennel, drizzle with the remaining dressing, and scatter the parsley and remaining mint over the top. Chop the reserved fronds and sprinkle over the salad.

GREAT TASTES MEDITERRANEAN

FRESH BEETROOT AND GOAT'S CHEESE SALAD

SERVES 4

1 kg (2 lb 4 oz) fresh beetroot (4 bulbs with leaves)
200 g (7 oz) green beans
1 tablespoon red wine vinegar
2 tablespoons extra virgin olive oil
1 garlic clove, crushed
1 tablespoon drained capers, coarsely chopped
½ teaspoon salt
½ teaspoon pepper
100 g (4 oz) goat's cheese

1 Trim the leaves from the beetroot. Scrub the bulbs and wash the leaves well. Add the whole bulbs to a large saucepan of salted water, bring to the boil, then reduce heat and simmer, covered, for 30 minutes, or until tender when pierced with the point of a knife.

2 Meanwhile, bring a pan of water to the boil, add the beans and cook for 3 minutes, or until just tender. Remove with a slotted spoon and plunge them into a bowl of cold water to stop the cooking process and retain their bright colour. Drain well. Add beetroot leaves to the same saucepan of water and cook for 3–5 minutes, or until the leaves and stems are tender. Drain, plunge into a bowl of cold water, then drain well.

3 Drain and cool the beetroots, then peel off the skins and cut the bulbs into thin wedges.

4 For the dressing, put the red wine vinegar, oil, garlic, capers, salt and pepper in a screw top jar and shake.

5 To serve, divide beans, beetroot leaves and bulbs among four serving plates. Crumble goat's cheese over the top and drizzle with dressing. Serve with fresh crusty bread.

FRISÉE AND GARLIC CROUTON SALAD

SERVES 4–6

VINAIGRETTE

1 French shallot, finely chopped

1 tablespoon Dijon mustard

¼ cup (60 ml/2 fl oz) tarragon vinegar

170 ml (6 fl oz/⅔ cup) extra virgin olive oil

1 tablespoon olive oil

250 g (8 oz) speck or smoked bacon, rind removed, cut into 5 mm x 2 cm (¼ x ¾ inch) pieces

½ medium bread stick, sliced

4 whole cloves garlic

1 baby frisée (curly endive), washed and dried

100 g (4 oz/½ cup) walnuts, toasted

1   For the vinaigrette, whisk together in a bowl the shallot, mustard and vinegar. Slowly add the oil, whisking constantly until thickened. Set aside.

2   Heat oil in a large frying pan, add speck, bread and garlic cloves and cook over a medium–high heat for 5–8 minutes, until the bread and speck are both crisp. Remove the garlic from the pan.

3   Place the frisée, bread, speck, walnuts and vinaigrette in a large bowl. Toss together well and serve.

GREEN BEANS WITH TOMATO AND OLIVE OIL

SERVES 4

80 ml (3 fl oz/⅓ cup) olive oil

1 large onion, chopped

3 garlic cloves, finely chopped

400 g (14 oz) tin chopped tomatoes

½ teaspoon sugar

750 g (1 lb 12 oz) green beans, trimmed

3 tablespoons chopped flat-leaf (Italian) parsley

1 Heat olive oil in a large frying pan, add the onion and cook over medium heat for 4–5 minutes, or until softened. Add the garlic and cook for another 30 seconds.

2 Add the tomato, sugar and 125 ml (4 fl oz/½ cup) water, then season with salt and freshly ground black pepper. Bring to the boil, then reduce the heat and simmer for 10 minutes, or until reduced slightly.

3 Add the beans and simmer for another 10 minutes, or until the beans are tender and the tomato mixture is pulpy. Stir in the parsley. Check the seasoning, and adjust according to your taste. Serve immediately, as a side dish.

TABBOULEH

SERVES 6

130 g (5 oz/¾ cup) burghul (bulgur)

3 ripe tomatoes

1 telegraph (long) cucumber

4 spring onions (scallions), sliced

120 g (4 oz/4 cups) chopped flat-leaf (Italian) parsley

25 g (1 oz/½ cup) chopped mint

DRESSING

80 ml (3 fl oz/⅓ cup) lemon juice

1½ teaspoon salt

60 ml (2 fl oz/¼ cup) olive oil

1 tablespoon extra virgin olive oil

1 **Place the burghul in a bowl,** cover with 500 ml (17 fl oz/ 2 cups) water and leave for 1½ hours.

2 **Cut the tomatoes in half,** squeeze gently to remove any excess seeds and cut into 1 cm (½ inch) cubes. Cut cucumber in half lengthways, remove the seeds with a teaspoon and cut the flesh into 1 cm (½ inch) cubes.

3 **To make the dressing,** place the lemon juice and salt in a bowl and whisk until well combined. Season well with freshly ground black pepper and slowly whisk in the olive oil and extra virgin olive oil.

4 **Drain the burghul** and squeeze out any excess water. Spread the burghul out on a clean tea towel or paper towels and leave to dry for about 30 minutes. Put the burghul in a large salad bowl, add the tomato, cucumber, spring onion, parsley and mint, and toss well to combine. Pour dressing over the salad and toss until evenly coated.

FATTOUSH

SERVES 6

2 pitta bread rounds (17 cm/7 inch diameter)

6 cos lettuce leaves, shredded

1 large Lebanese (short) cucumber, cut into 1 cm (½ inch) cubes

4 ripe tomatoes, cut into 1 cm (½ inch) cubes

8 spring onions (scallions), chopped

4 tablespoons chopped flat-leaf (Italian) parsley

1 tablespoon chopped fresh mint

2 tablespoons chopped fresh coriander

DRESSING

2 garlic cloves, crushed

100 ml (4 fl oz) extra virgin olive oil

100 ml (4 fl oz) lemon juice

1 **Preheat oven** to 180°C (350°F/Gas 4). Split the bread into two through the centre and bake on a baking tray for about 8 minutes, or until golden and crisp, turning halfway through. Break into small pieces.

2 **For the dressing,** whisk all the ingredients together in a bowl until combined.

3 **Place the bread pieces** and remaining salad ingredients in a bowl and toss. Pour on the dressing and toss well. Season, to taste, with salt and ground black pepper. Serve immediately.

ROASTED BALSAMIC ONIONS

SERVES 8 (AS PART OF AN ANTIPASTO PLATTER)

1 kg (2 lb 4 oz) baby onions, unpeeled (see Note)

185 ml (6 fl oz/¾ cup) balsamic vinegar

2 tablespoons soft brown sugar

185 ml (6 fl oz/¾ cup) olive oil

1 Preheat the oven to 160°C (315°F/Gas 2–3). Bake the onions in a baking dish for 1½ hours. When cool enough to handle, trim the stems from the onions and peel away the skin (the outer part of the root should come away but the onions will remain intact). Rinse a 1 litre (35 fl oz/4 cup) wide-necked jar with boiling water and dry in a warm oven (do not dry with a tea towel). Add the onions to the jar.

2 Combine the vinegar and sugar in a small screw top jar and stir to dissolve the sugar. Add the oil, seal the jar and shake the jar vigorously until the mixture is combined.

3 Pour the vinegar mixture over the onions, seal, and turn upside-down to coat. Marinate overnight in the refrigerator, turning occasionally. Return to room temperature and shake to combine the dressing before serving.

Note: Baby onions are very small. An ideal size is around 35 g (1 oz) each. Sizes will probably range from 20 g (¾ oz) up to 40 g (1½ oz). The cooking time given is suitable for this range and there is no need to cook the larger ones for any longer. The marinating time given is a minimum time and the onions can be marinated up to three days in the refrigerator. The marinade may separate after a few hours, which is fine — simply stir occasionally.

ARTICHOKES VINAIGRETTE

SERVES 4

2 tablespoons lemon juice

4 young Romanesco or Violetto Toscano artichokes

good-quality ready-made vinaigrette

1 **Mix the lemon juice** in a large bowl with 1 litre (35 fl oz/ 4 cups) cold water. Using kitchen scissors or a sharp knife, cut off and discard the top third of each artichoke. Discard the tough outer leaves and snip off any spikes from the remaining leaves. Chop off and discard all but 2–3 cm (¾–1¼ inch) of the stem and peel this with a potato peeler.

2 **Slice each artichoke in half** from the top to the bottom, including the stem. Scrape out the furry choke and discard. As each artichoke is prepared, place it straight into the bowl of lemon water to avoid discolouring.

3 **Shake each artichoke half dry** and arrange on a serving platter. Spoon the vinaigrette over the top and leave for at least 30 minutes before serving.

ʹOUILLE

SERVES 4

4 tomatoes

2 tablespoons olive oil

1 large onion, diced

1 red capsicum (pepper), diced

1 yellow capsicum (pepper), diced

1 eggplant (aubergine), diced

2 zucchini (courgettes), diced

1 teaspoon tomato paste (concentrated purée)

½ teaspoon sugar

1 bay leaf

3 sprigs of thyme

2 sprigs of basil

1 garlic clove, crushed

1 tablespoon chopped parsley

1 **Score a cross** in the top of each tomato, plunge tomatoes into boiling water for 20 seconds and then peel the skin away from the cross. Chop flesh roughly.

2 **Heat the oil** in a frying pan. Add the onion and cook over low heat for 5 minutes. Add the capsicums and cook, stirring, for 4 minutes. Remove from the pan and set aside.

3 **Fry the eggplant** until lightly browned all over and then remove from the pan. Fry zucchini until browned. Return the onion, capsicums and eggplant to the pan. Add the tomato paste, stir well and cook for 2 minutes. Add tomato, sugar, bay leaf, thyme and basil, stir well, cover and cook for 15 minutes. Remove the bay leaf, thyme and basil.

4 **Combine the garlic** and parsley and add to the ratatouille at the last minute. Stir and serve.

GREAT TASTES MEDITERRANEAN

CRISP POTATOES IN SPICY TOMATO SAUCE

SERVES 6

1 kg (2 lb 4 oz) desiree potatoes
oil, for deep-frying
500 g (1 lb 2 oz) ripe roma (plum) tomatoes
2 tablespoons olive oil
¼ red onion, finely chopped
2 garlic cloves, crushed
3 teaspoons paprika
¼ teaspoon cayenne pepper
1 bay leaf
1 teaspoon sugar
1 tablespoon chopped flat-leaf (Italian) parsley, to garnish

1 **Cut potatoes** into 2 cm (¾ inch) cubes. Rinse, then drain well and pat completely dry. Fill a deep-fryer or large heavy-based saucepan one third full of oil and heat to 180°C (350°F), or until a cube of bread dropped into the oil browns in 15 seconds. Cook potato in batches for 10 minutes, or until golden. Drain well on paper towels. Do not discard the oil.

2 **Score a cross** in the base of each tomato. Place in a bowl of boiling water for 20 seconds, then plunge into cold water and peel the skin away from the cross. Chop the flesh.

3 **Heat the olive oil** in a saucepan over medium heat and cook the onion for 3 minutes, or until softened. Add the garlic, paprika and cayenne and cook for 1–2 minutes, until fragrant.

4 **Add tomato,** bay leaf, sugar and 90 ml (3 fl oz/⅓ cup) water, and cook, stirring occasionally, for 20 minutes, or until thick and pulpy. Cool slightly and remove the bay leaf. Blend in a food processor until smooth, adding a little water if necessary. Before serving, return the sauce to the saucepan and simmer over low heat for 2 minutes, or until heated though. Season well.

5 **Reheat the oil** to 180°C (350°F). Re-cook the potato, in batches, for 2 minutes, or until very crisp and golden. Drain on paper towels. This second frying makes the potato extra crispy and stops the sauce soaking in immediately. Place on a platter and cover with sauce. Garnish with parsley and serve.

FRIED CHICKPEAS

SERVES 6

275 g (10 oz/1¼ cups) dried chickpeas

oil, for deep-frying

½ teaspoon paprika

¼ teaspoon cayenne pepper

1 Soak the chickpeas overnight in plenty of cold water. Drain well and pat dry with paper towels.

2 Fill a deep saucepan one third full of oil and heat to 180°C (350°F), or until a cube of bread dropped into the oil browns in 15 seconds. Deep-fry half the chickpeas for 3 minutes, remove them from pan with a slotted spoon and drain on crumpled paper towels. Repeat with remaining chickpeas. Partially cover the saucepan as some of the chickpeas may pop. Don't leave the oil unattended.

3 Deep-fry the chickpeas again in batches for 3 minutes each batch, or until browned. Drain well again on crumpled paper towels. Combine the paprika and cayenne pepper with a little salt and sprinkle the mixture over the hot chickpeas. Allow to cool before serving.

WARM PUMPKIN SALAD WITH PRESERVED LEMON

SERVES 4

1 kg (2 lb 4 oz) firm pumpkin (winter squash) or butternut pumpkin (squash)

1 preserved lemon (available in jars at delicatessens and Middle Eastern supermarkets)

3 tablespoons olive oil

1 brown onion, grated

½ teaspoon ground ginger

½ teaspoon ground cumin

1 teaspoon paprika

2 tablespoons chopped flat-leaf (Italian) parsley

2 tablespoons chopped coriander (cilantro) leaves

1 tablespoon lemon juice

1 **Peel pumpkin,** remove seeds and cut into 2 cm (¾ inch) chunks. Set aside. Remove pulp from preserved lemon, rinse rind, dice and set aside.

2 **Heat olive oil** in a large, lidded frying pan on medium heat and add onion. Cook for 3 minutes, stir in ginger, cumin and paprika and cook for a further 30 seconds. Add the pumpkin, parsley, coriander, lemon juice, preserved lemon and 125 ml (4 fl oz/½ cup) water. Season to taste, cover and simmer on low heat for 20 minutes until tender, tossing occasionally with a spatula, adding a little more water if necessary. Serve warm as an appetiser or hot as a vegetable accompaniment.

BAKED EGGPLANT WITH TOMATO AND MOZZARELLA

SERVES 6

6 large slender eggplants (aubergines), cut in half lengthways, leaving stems attached

5 tablespoons olive oil

2 onions, finely chopped

2 garlic cloves, crushed

400 g (14 oz) tin chopped tomatoes

1 tablespoon tomato paste (concentrated purée)

3 tablespoons chopped flat-leaf (Italian) parsley

1 tablespoon chopped fresh oregano

125 g (5 oz) mozzarella, grated

1 **Preheat the oven** to moderate 180°C (350°F/Gas 4). Score the eggplant flesh by cutting a criss-cross pattern with a sharp knife, taking care not to cut right through the skin. Then heat 2 tablespoons of the oil in a large frying pan, add 3 eggplants and cook for 2–3 minutes each side, or until the flesh is soft. Remove. Repeat with another 2 tablespoons of the oil and the remaining eggplants. Cool slightly; scoop out the flesh, leaving a 2 mm (⅛ inch) border. Finely chop flesh. Reserve the shells.

2 **In the same pan,** heat the remaining oil and cook the onion over medium heat for 5 minutes. Add the garlic and cook for 30 seconds, then add tomato, tomato paste, herbs and eggplant flesh, and cook, stirring occasionally, over low heat for 8–10 minutes, or until the sauce is thick and pulpy. Season well.

3 **Arrange the eggplant shells** in a lightly greased baking dish and spoon in the tomato filling. Sprinkle with mozzarella and bake for 5–10 minutes, or until the cheese has melted.

BAKED CAPSICUMS WITH ANCHOVIES

SERVES 6

3 yellow capsicums (peppers)
3 red capsicums (peppers)
2 tablespoons extra virgin olive oil
12 anchovy fillets, halved lengthways
3 garlic cloves, thinly sliced
25 g (1 oz/½ cup) basil leaves
1 tablespoon baby capers, rinsed
extra virgin olive oil, for serving

1   **Preheat oven** to 180°C (350°F/Gas 4). Cut each capsicum in half lengthways, leaving the stems intact. If the capsicums are large, quarter them. Remove the seeds and membrane. Drizzle a little of the oil in a baking dish and place capsicums in, skin-side-down. Season with salt and pepper.

2   **In each capsicum,** place a halved anchovy fillet, slivers of garlic and a torn basil leaf. Divide the capers among the capsicums. Season with salt and pepper and drizzle with the remaining oil.

3   **Cover dish with foil** and bake capsicums for 20 minutes. Remove the foil and cook for another 25–30 minutes, or until the capsicums are tender. Drizzle with a little extra virgin olive oil. Scatter the remaining torn basil leaves over the capsicums and serve warm or at room temperature.

DESSERTS

ALMOND SHORTBREADS

MAKES 22

250 g (9 oz) unsalted butter

100 g (4 oz) slivered almonds

250 g (9 oz/2 cups) plain (all-purpose) flour

1 teaspoon baking powder

90 g (3 oz/¾ cup) icing (confectioners') sugar, sifted

1 egg yolk

1 teaspoon natural vanilla extract

1 tablespoon ouzo

4 tablespoons almond meal

60 g (2 oz/½ cup) icing (confectioners') sugar, extra, for dusting

1 **Gently melt the butter** over low heat in a small heavy-based saucepan, without stirring or shaking the pan. Carefully pour the clear butter into another container, leaving the white sediment in the pan to be discarded. Refrigerate for 1 hour.

2 **Preheat the oven** to 170°C (325°F/Gas 3) and line two baking trays with baking paper. Grind the slivered almonds to a medium-fine meal. In a bowl, sift the flour and baking powder together.

3 **Using electric beaters,** beat the chilled butter until light and fluffy. Gradually add the icing sugar and combine well. Add the egg yolk, vanilla and ouzo and beat until just combined. Fold in the flour, ground almonds and the almond meal.

4 **Shape heaped tablespoons** of mixture into crescents, place on the baking trays and bake for 12 minutes, or until lightly coloured. Remove from the oven and dust liberally with icing sugar. Leave to cool on the trays for 10 minutes.

5 **Line a baking tray** with baking paper and dust the paper with icing sugar. Lift warm biscuits onto this and dust again with icing sugar. When biscuits are cool, dust them again with icing sugar before storing them in an airtight container.

SHREDDED PASTRIES WITH ALMONDS

MAKES 40 PIECES

500 g (1 lb 2 oz) kataifi pastry (see Note)

250 g (9 oz) unsalted butter, melted

125 g (4 oz/1 cup) ground pistachios

230 g (8 oz/2 cups) ground almonds

625 g (1 lb 6 oz/2½ cups) caster (superfine) sugar

1 teaspoon ground cinnamon

¼ teaspoon ground cloves

1 tablespoon brandy

1 egg white

1 teaspoon lemon juice

5 cm (2 inch) strip lemon zest

4 cloves

1 cinnamon stick

1 tablespoon honey

1   Bring **kataifi pastry** to room temperature, in its packaging. It will take 2 hours and makes the pastry easier to work with.

2   **Preheat oven** to 170°C (325°/Gas 3). Brush a 20 x 30 cm (8 x 12 inch) baking dish or tray with melted butter.

3   **Place the nuts in a bowl** with 125 g (5 oz/½ cup) caster sugar, the ground cinnamon, cloves and brandy. Lightly beat the egg white with a fork and add to the mixture. Stir to make a paste. Divide the mixture into 8 portions and form each into a sausage shape about 18 cm (7 inches) long.

4   **Take a small handful** of pastry strands and lay them out fairly compactly with strands running lengthways towards you. Pastry should measure 25 x 18 cm (10 x 7 inches). Brush with melted butter. Place one of the 'nut' sausages along the end of the pastry nearest you and roll up into a neat sausage shape. Repeat with the other pastry portions.

5   **Place the rolls** close together in the baking dish and brush them again with melted butter. Bake for 50 minutes, or until golden brown While the pastries are cooking, place the remaining sugar in a small saucepan with 500 ml (17 fl oz/ 2 cups) water and stir over low heat until dissolved. Add the lemon juice, rind, cloves and cinnamon and boil together for 10 minutes. Stir in the honey, then set aside until cold.

6   **When pastries** come out of the oven, pour syrup over the top. Leave to cool completely, then cut each roll into 5 pieces.

Notes: Kataifi, a shredded pastry, is available from Greek delicatessens and other speciality food stores. Make sure that the syrup is cold and the kataifi hot when pouring the syrup over, otherwise it will not be absorbed as well. These pastries keep for up to a week if covered. Don't refrigerate them.

SEMOLINA CAKE

SERVES 6–8

SYRUP
625 g (1 lb 6 oz/2½ cups) sugar

2 tablespoons lemon juice

125 g (5 oz) unsalted butter

185 g (7 oz/¾ cup) caster (superfine) sugar

2 teaspoons finely grated lemon zest

3 eggs

185 g (7 oz/1½ cups) semolina

125 g (5 oz/1 cup) self-raising flour

125 ml (4 fl oz/½ cup) milk

80 g (3 oz/½ cup) blanched almonds, toasted and finely chopped

blanched flaked almonds, to decorate

1   Preheat the oven to 170°C (325°F/Gas 3). Grease a 30 x 20 cm (12 x 8 inch) cake tin.

2   In a saucepan, dissolve the sugar in 750 g (24 fl oz/3 cups) water over high heat, add the lemon juice and bring to the boil. Reduce the heat to medium and simmer for 20 minutes. Remove from the heat and leave until cool.

3   While the syrup is cooking, cream the butter, sugar and lemon zest with electric beaters until light and fluffy. Add the eggs one at a time, beating well after each addition.

4   Sift together the semolina and flour and fold into butter mixture alternately with the milk. Mix in the chopped almonds, then spread the mixture into the tin and arrange rows of flaked almonds on top. Bake for 35–40 minutes, or until the cake is golden and shrinks slightly from the sides of the tin. Prick the surface with a fine skewer, then pour cooled syrup over the hot cake. When cake is cool, cut it into squares or diamonds.

YOGHURT CAKE WITH SYRUP

185 g (6 oz) unsalted butter, softened

250 g (9 oz/1 cup) caster (superfine) sugar

5 eggs, separated

250 g (9 oz/1 cup) Greek-style natural yoghurt

2 teaspoons grated lemon rind

½ teaspoon natural vanilla extract

280 g (9 oz/2¼ cups) plain (all-purpose) flour

½ teaspoon bicarbonate of soda (baking soda)

2 teaspoons baking powder

whipped cream, for serving

SYRUP

250 g (9 oz/1 cup) caster sugar

1 cinnamon stick

4 cm (1½ inch) strip lemon zest

1 tablespoon lemon juice

1   Preheat the oven to 180°C (350°F/Gas 4) and lightly grease a 20 x 10 cm (8 x 4 inch) loaf tin.

2   Cream butter and sugar in a bowl with electric beaters until light and fluffy. Add the egg yolks gradually, beating well after each addition. Stir in the yoghurt, lemon zest and vanilla essence. Fold in sifted flour, bicarbonate of soda and baking powder with a metal spoon.

3   Whisk the egg whites in a clean, dry bowl until stiff and gently fold into the mixture. Spoon into the tin and bake for 50 minutes, or until a skewer comes out clean when inserted into the centre of the cake. Cool in the tin for 10 minutes, then turn out onto a wire rack.

4   Meanwhile, for the syrup, place the sugar and cinnamon stick in a small saucepan with 185 ml (6 fl oz/¾ cup) cold water. Stir over medium heat until the sugar has dissolved. Bring to the boil, add the lemon rind and juice, then reduce the heat and simmer for 5–6 minutes. Strain, then pour syrup all over the hot cake and wait for most of it to be absorbed before you serve the cake. Serve warm with whipped cream.

BAKLAVA

MAKES 18 PIECES

560 g (11 lb 4 oz/2¼ cups) caster (superfine) sugar

1½ teaspoons grated lemon zest

90 g (3 oz/¼ cup) honey

60 ml (2 fl oz/¼ cup) lemon juice

2 tablespoons orange blossom water

200 g (7 oz) walnuts, finely chopped

200 g (7 oz) shelled pistachios, finely chopped

200 g (7 oz) almonds, finely chopped

2 tablespoons caster (superfine) sugar, extra

2 teaspoons ground cinnamon

200 g (7 oz) unsalted butter, melted

375 g (12 oz) ready-made filo pastry

1 **Place the sugar,** lemon zest and 375 ml (12 fl oz/1½ cups) water in a saucepan and stir over high heat until the sugar has dissolved, then boil for 5 minutes. Reduce the heat to low and simmer for 5 minutes, or until the syrup has thickened slightly and just coats the back of a spoon. Add the honey, lemon juice and orange blossom water and cook for 2 minutes. Remove from the heat and leave to cool completely.

2 **Preheat the oven** to 170°C (325°F/Gas 3). Combine the nuts, extra sugar and cinnamon in a bowl. Brush the base and sides of a 30 x 27 cm (12 x 11 inch) baking dish or tin with the melted butter. Cover the base with a single layer of filo pastry, brush lightly with the butter, folding in any overhanging edges. Continue layering the filo, brushing each new layer with butter and folding in the edges until 10 sheets have been used. Keep the unused filo under a damp tea towel.

3 **Sprinkle half the nut mixture** over the pastry and pat down evenly. Repeat the layering and buttering of 5 more filo sheets, sprinkle with the remaining nuts, then continue to layer and butter the remaining sheets, including the top layer. Press down with your hands so the pastry and nuts adhere to each other. Cut into diamond shapes, ensuring you cut through to the base. Pour any remaining butter evenly over the top and smooth. Bake for 30 minutes, then lower the temperature to 150°C (300°F/Gas 2) and cook for another 30 minutes.

4 **Immediately cut through** the original diamond markings, then strain the syrup evenly over the top. Cool completely before lifting the diamonds out onto a serving platter.

Note: To achieve the right texture, make sure the baklava is piping hot and the syrup cold when pouring the syrup.

SERVES 4

100 g (4 oz) blanched whole almonds
12 whole fresh figs (about 750 g/ 1 lb 10 oz)
125 g (5 oz/½ cup) sugar
115 g (4 oz/⅓ cup) honey
2 tablespoons lemon juice
6 cm (2½ inch) sliver of lemon zest
1 cinnamon stick
250 g (9 oz/1 cup) Greek-style natural yoghurt

1 **Preheat oven** to 180°C (350°F/Gas 4). Place the almonds on a baking tray and bake for 5 minutes, or until golden. Leave to cool. Cut the stems off the figs and make a small crossways incision 5 mm (¼ inch) deep on top of each one. Push a blanched almond in the base of each fig. Roughly chop the remaining almonds.

2 **Place 750 ml** (25 fl oz/3 cups) water in a large saucepan, add the sugar and stir over medium heat until sugar dissolves. Increase heat and bring to the boil. Stir in the honey, lemon juice, lemon rind and cinnamon stick. Reduce heat to medium, place the figs in the pan and simmer gently for 30 minutes. Remove with a slotted spoon. Place on a large serving dish.

3 **Boil liquid** over high heat for about 15–20 minutes, or until thick and syrupy. Remove cinnamon and rind. Cool the syrup slightly and pour over the figs. Sprinkle with the almonds and serve warm or cold with yoghurt

...ERRIES WITH BALSAMIC VINEGAR

750 g (1 lb 10 oz) ripe small strawberries

60 g (2 oz/¼ cup) caster (superfine) sugar

2 tablespoons good-quality balsamic vinegar

125 g (5 oz/½ cup) mascarpone, to serve

1 **Wipe the strawberries** with a clean damp cloth and hull them. Halve large strawberries.

2 **Place the strawberries in a glass bowl,** sprinkle the sugar evenly over the top and toss gently to coat. Leave for 30 minutes to macerate. Sprinkle the vinegar over the strawberries, toss and refrigerate for 30 minutes.

3 **Spoon the strawberries** into four glasses, drizzle with the syrup and top with a dollop of mascarpone.

STUFFED PEACHES

SERVES 6

6 ripe peaches

60 g (2 oz) amaretti biscuits, crushed

1 egg yolk

2 tablespoons caster (superfine) sugar

20 g (1 oz) almond meal

1 tablespoon amaretto

60 ml (2 fl oz/¼ cup) white wine

1 teaspoon caster (superfine) sugar, extra

20 g (1 oz) unsalted butter

1 **Preheat the oven** to 180°C (350°/Gas 4) and lightly grease a 30 x 25 cm (12 x 10 inch) ovenproof dish with butter.

2 **Cut each peach in half** and carefully remove the stones. Scoop a little of the pulp out from each and combine in a small bowl with the crushed biscuits, egg yolk, caster sugar, almond meal and amaretto.

3 **Spoon some of the mixture** into each peach and place them cut-side-up in the dish. Sprinkle with the white wine and the extra sugar. Place a dot of butter on the top of each and bake for 20–25 minutes, until golden.

Note: When they are in season, you can also use ripe apricots or nectarines for this recipe.

CATALAN CUSTARD

SERVES 6

1 litre (35 fl oz/4 cups) milk

1 vanilla bean, split

1 cinnamon stick

zest of 1 small lemon, cut into strips

2 strips orange zest, 4 x 2 cm
  (1½ x ¾ inch)

8 egg yolks

115 g (4 oz/½ cup) caster (superfine)
  sugar

40 g (1½ oz/⅓ cup) cornflour
  (cornstarch)

45 g (1½ oz/¼ cup) soft brown sugar

1 **Put the milk,** scraped vanilla bean, cinnamon stick and lemon and orange zests in a saucepan and bring to the boil. Simmer for 5 minutes, then strain and set aside.

2 **Whisk egg yolks** with the sugar in a bowl for 5 minutes, or until pale and creamy. Add the cornflour and mix well. Slowly add the warm milk mixture to the egg while you whisk continuously. Return to the saucepan and cook over low–medium heat, stirring constantly, for 5–10 minutes, or until the mixture is thick and creamy. Do not allow it to boil as it will curdle. Pour into six 185 ml (6 fl oz/¾ cup) ramekins and refrigerate for 6 hours, or overnight.

3 **When ready to serve,** sprinkle the top evenly with brown sugar and grill (broil) for 3 minutes, or until it caramelises.

CHURROS

SERVES 4

125 g (5 oz/½ cup) sugar
1 teaspoon ground nutmeg
30 g (1 oz) butter
150 g (6 oz) plain (all-purpose) flour
½ teaspoon finely grated orange zest
¼ teaspoon caster (superfine) sugar
2 eggs
1 litre (35 fl oz/4 cups) vegetable oil, for deep-frying

1 **Combine sugar and nutmeg** and spread out on a plate.

2 **Place the butter,** flour, orange rind, caster sugar, 170 ml (6 fl oz/⅔ cup) water and a pinch of salt in a heavy-based saucepan. Stir over a low heat until the butter softens and combines with the other ingredients to form a dough. Keep cooking for 2–3 minutes, stirring constantly, until the dough forms a ball around the spoon and leaves a coating on the base of the pan.

3 **Transfer the dough** to a food processor and, with the motor running, add the eggs. Do not over-process. If dough is too soft to snip with scissors, return it to the pan and cook, stirring over low heat until it is firmer. Spoon it into a piping bag fitted with a 5 mm (¼ inch) star nozzle.

4 **Heat the oil** in a wide saucepan to 180°C (350°F) or when a cube of bread dropped into the oil browns in 15 seconds. Pipe lengths of batter 6–8 cm (2½–3 inches) long into the oil a few at a time. An easy technique is to pipe with one hand and cut the batter off with kitchen scissors in the other hand. Fry for about 3 minutes, until puffed and golden, turning once or twice. Transfer each batch to paper towels to drain. While still hot, toss them in the sugar mixture and serve at once.

Note: Churros is a popular breakfast snack in Spain and is usually eaten with hot chocolate.

FRIED HONEY CAKES

SERVES 4-6

3 eggs

60 ml (2 fl oz/¼ cup) orange juice

60 ml (2 fl oz/¼ cup) vegetable oil

1 tablespoon grated orange rind

60 g (2 oz/¼ cup) caster (superfine) sugar

300 g (10 oz) plain (all-purpose) flour

1 teaspoon baking powder

about 4 tablespoons flour, extra, for rolling

SYRUP

2 tablespoons lemon juice

275 g (10 oz) sugar

115 g (4 oz/⅓ cup) honey

1 tablespoon grated orange zest

vegetable oil, for deep-frying

1 Whisk eggs, orange juice and oil together in a large bowl. Add orange rind and sugar and whisk until frothy. Sift in the flour and baking powder and mix with a wooden spoon until smooth, but still a bit sticky. Cover and set aside for 1 hour.

2 To make the syrup, heat 315 ml (11 fl oz/1¼ cups) cold water in a saucepan with the lemon juice and sugar, stirring until the sugar dissolves. Bring to the boil, reduce the heat and simmer for 5 minutes. Add the honey and orange rind and simmer for another 5 minutes. Keep warm.

3 Sprinkle a little of the extra flour onto the dough and transfer it to a lightly floured surface. Work in just enough extra flour to give a dough which doesn't stick to your hands. Roll it out to a thickness of 5 mm (¼ inch). It will be very elastic, so keep rolling and resting it until it stops shrinking. Using a 5 cm (2 inch) biscuit cutter, cut out round cakes.

4 Heat the oil in a large deep-sided frying pan to 170°C (325°F), or until a cube of bread dropped into the oil browns in 20 seconds. Fry the cakes 3 or 4 at a time until puffed and golden, about 1 minute on each side. Remove with tongs and drain on paper towels.

5 With tongs, dip each cake into warm syrup long enough for it to soak in. Transfer to a plate. Serve warm or cold.

GREAT TASTES MEDITERRANEAN

ISRAELI DOUGHNUTS

MAKES 14

185 ml (6 fl oz/¾ cup) lukewarm milk

1 tablespoon dried yeast

2 tablespoons caster (superfine) sugar

375 g (13 oz/2½ cups) plain (all-purpose) flour

2 teaspoons ground cinnamon

1 teaspoon finely grated lemon zest

2 eggs, separated

40 g (1¼ oz) butter, softened

100 g (4 oz/⅓ cup) plum, strawberry or apricot jam or conserve

oil, for deep-frying

caster (superfine) sugar, extra, for rolling

1 Put the milk in a small bowl, add yeast and 1 tablespoon of the sugar and leave in a warm place for 10 minutes, or until bubbles appear on the surface. If your yeast doesn't foam, it is 'dead' and you will have to start again.

2 Sift the flour into a large bowl and add the cinnamon, lemon rind, egg yolks, yeast mixture, remaining sugar, and a pinch of salt. Mix well, then place the dough on a lightly floured work surface and knead for 5 minutes. Work in the butter, a little at a time, continually kneading until the dough becomes elastic. This will take about 10 minutes. Place in a large bowl and cover with a clean, damp tea towel (dish towel). Leave to rise overnight in the refrigerator.

3 Place dough on a lightly floured work surface. Roll out to 3 mm (⅛ inch) thickness. Using a 6 cm (2½ inch) cutter, cut 28 rounds from the dough. Place 14 of the rounds on a lightly floured tray and carefully place ¾ teaspoon of the jam or conserve into the centre of each. Lightly beat the egg whites, then brush a little around the outside edges of the rounds, being careful not to touch the jam at all. Top with the remaining 14 rounds and press down firmly around the edges to seal. Cover with a clean tea towel and leave to rise for 30 minutes. Make sure the dough has not separated at the edges. Press any open edges firmly together.

4 Fill a deep heavy-based saucepan one third full of oil and heat to 170°C (325°F), or until a cube of bread dropped into the oil browns in 20 seconds. Cook the doughnuts in batches for 1½ minutes on both sides, or until golden. Drain on crumpled paper towels and roll in caster sugar. Serve immediately.

PANFORTE

MAKES ONE 23 CM (9 INCH) CAKE

105 g (4 oz/¾ cup) hazelnuts

115 g (4½ oz/¾ cup) almonds

125 g (5 oz) candied mixed peel, chopped

100 g (4 oz) candied pineapple, chopped

grated zest of 1 lemon

80 g (3 oz/⅔ cup) plain (all-purpose) flour

1 teaspoon ground cinnamon

¼ teaspoon ground coriander

¼ teaspoon ground cloves

¼ teaspoon grated nutmeg

pinch of white pepper

140 g (5½ oz/⅔ cup) sugar

4 tablespoons honey

50 g (2 oz) unsalted butter

icing (confectioners') sugar

1 Line a 23 cm (9 inch) springform tin with rice paper or baking parchment and grease well with butter. Toast the nuts under a hot grill (broiler), turning them so they brown on all sides, then leave to cool. Put the nuts in a bowl with the mixed peel, pineapple, lemon zest, flour and spices and toss together. Preheat the oven to 150°C (300°F/Gas 2).

2 Put the sugar, honey and butter in a saucepan and melt them together. Cook the syrup until it reaches 120°C (250°F) on a sugar thermometer, or a little of it dropped into cold water forms a soft ball when moulded between your finger and thumb.

3 Pour the syrup into the nut mixture and mix well, working fast before it stiffens too much. Pour it straight into the tin, smooth the surface and bake for 35 minutes. (Unlike other cakes, this will not firm up as it cooks, nor will it colour at all, so you need to time it carefully.)

4 Cool in the tin until the cake firms up enough to remove the side of the tin. Peel off the paper. Leave to cool completely. Dust the top heavily with icing sugar.

LEMON GELATO

SERVES 6

5 egg yolks

110 g (4 oz/½ cup) sugar

500 ml (17 fl oz/2 cups) milk

2 tablespoons grated lemon zest

185 ml (6 fl oz/¾ cup) lemon juice

3 tablespoons thick (double/heavy) cream

1 Whisk the egg yolks and half the sugar together until pale and creamy. Place the milk, lemon zest and remaining sugar in a saucepan and bring to the boil. Pour over the egg mixture and whisk to combine. Pour the custard back into the saucepan and cook over low heat, stirring continuously until the mixture is thick enough to coat the back of a wooden spoon—do not allow the custard to boil.

2 Strain the custard into a bowl, add the lemon juice and cream and then cool over ice. Churn in an ice-cream maker following the manufacturer's instructions. Or, pour custard into a plastic freezer box, cover and freeze. Stir every 30 minutes with a whisk during freezing to break up the ice crystals and give a better texture. Keep in the freezer until ready to serve.

CRÈME CARAMEL

SERVES 6

CARAMEL

115 g (4 oz/½ cup) caster (superfine)
　sugar

625 ml (22 fl oz/2½ cups) milk

1 vanilla pod

125 g (5 oz/½ cup) caster (superfine)
　sugar

3 eggs, beaten

3 egg yolks

1　To make the caramel, put the sugar in a heavy-based saucepan and heat until it dissolves and starts to caramelize—tip the saucepan from side to side to keep the colouring even. Remove from the heat and carefully add 2 tablespoons water to stop the cooking process. Pour into six 125 ml (4 fl oz/½ cup) ramekins and leave to cool.

2　Preheat oven to 180°C (350°F/Gas 4). Put the milk and vanilla pod in a saucepan and bring just to the boil. Combine the sugar, eggs and egg yolks. Strain the boiling milk over the egg mixture and stir well. Ladle into ramekins and place in a roasting tin. Pour enough hot water into the tin to come halfway up the sides of the ramekins. Cook for 35–40 minutes, or until custards are firm to the touch. Remove from the tin and leave for 15 minutes. Unmould onto plates. Pour any leftover caramel over the top.

MIXED BERRY TARTLETS

MAKES 10

FRANGIPANE

250 g (9 oz) unsalted butter

250 g (9 oz/2 cups) icing (confectioners') sugar

230 g (8 oz/2¼ cups) ground almonds

40 g (1¼ oz/⅓ cup) plain (all-purpose) flour

5 eggs, lightly beaten

SWEET PASTRY

340 g (11½ oz/2¾ cups) plain (all-purpose) flour

a pinch of salt

150 g (5½ oz) unsalted butter

90 g (3 oz/¾ cup) icing (confectioners') sugar

2 eggs, beaten

400 g (14 oz) mixed berries

3 tablespoons apricot jam (jelly)

1 To make the frangipane, beat the butter until very soft. Add the icing sugar, ground almonds and flour and beat well. Add the egg gradually, beating until fully incorporated. Transfer to a clean bowl, cover with plastic wrap and refrigerate for up to 24 hours.

2 To make the pastry, sift the flour and salt onto a work surface and make a well in the centre. Put the butter in the well and work, using a pecking action with your fingertips and thumb, until it is very soft. Add the sugar and mix into the butter. Add eggs and combine. Gradually incorporate the flour, flicking it onto the mixture and then chopping through it until you have a rough dough. Bring together with your hands and then knead a few times to make a smooth dough. Roll into a ball, wrap in plastic wrap and leave in the refrigerator for at least 1 hour.

3 Preheat the oven to 180°C (350°F/Gas 4). Roll out pastry on a lightly floured surfacte to a thickness of 2 mm (⅛ inch) and use to line ten 8 cm (3 inch) wide tartlet tins. Put the frangipane in a piping bag and pipe into tartlet tins. Put tins on a baking tray and bake for 10–12 minutes, or until golden.

4 Cool slightly on a wire rack, then arrange the berries on top. Melt the jam with 1 teaspoon water over a low heat, sieve out any lumps and brush over the berries to make them shine.

TIRAMISU

SERVES 4

5 eggs, separated

170 g (6 oz/¾ cup) caster (superfine) sugar

300 g (11 oz) mascarpone cheese

250 ml (9 fl oz/1 cup) cold strong coffee

3 tablespoons brandy or sweet Marsala

36 small sponge fingers

80 g (3 oz) dark chocolate, finely grated

1 Beat the egg yolks with the sugar until the sugar has dissolved and the mixture is light and fluffy and leaves a ribbon trail when dropped from the whisk. Add the mascarpone and beat until the mixture is smooth.

2 Whisk the egg whites in a clean dry glass bowl, using a wire whisk or hand beaters, until soft peaks form. Fold into the mascarpone mixture.

3 Pour the coffee into a shallow dish and add the brandy. Dip enough biscuits to cover the base of a 25 cm (10 inch) square dish into the coffee. The biscuits should be fairly well soaked but not so much so that they break up. Arrange the biscuits in one tightly packed layer in the base of the dish.

4 Spread half of the mascarpone mixture over the layer of biscuits. Add another layer of soaked biscuits and top with another layer of mascarpone, smoothing the top layer neatly.

5 Dust with the grated chocolate to serve.

Note: The flavours will be better developed if you can make the tiramisu a few hours in advance or even the night before. If you have time to do this, don't dust with the chocolate, but cover with plastic wrap and chill. Dust with chocolate at the last minute.

CANNOLI

PASTRY

155 g (6 oz/1¼ cups) plain (all-purpose) flour

2 teaspoons cocoa powder

1 teaspoon instant coffee

1 tablespoon caster (superfine) sugar

25 g (1 oz) unsalted butter, chilled and cut into small cubes

3 tablespoons dry white wine

1 teaspoon dry Marsala (or dry sherry)

1 egg, beaten

oil for deep-frying

FILLING

300 g (11 oz) ricotta cheese

145 g (5 oz/⅔ cup) caster (superfine) sugar

¼ teaspoon natural vanilla extract

½ teaspoon grated lemon zest

1 tablespoon candied peel, finely chopped

6 glacé cherries, chopped

15 g (½ oz) dark chocolate, grated

icing (confectioners') sugar

1 To make the pastry, mix the flour, cocoa powder, coffee and sugar in a bowl. Rub in the butter, then add the wine and Marsala and mix until the dough gathers into a loose clump. Transfer dough to a lightly floured surface and knead until smooth (the dough will be quite stiff). Chill in a plastic bag for 30 minutes.

2 Lightly dust the work surface with flour and roll the pastry out to about 32 x 24 cm (13 x 9 inch). Trim the edges, then cut the pastry into twelve 8 cm (3 inch) squares. Lightly oil the metal cannoli tubes. Wrap a pastry square diagonally around each tube, securing the overlapping corners with beaten egg and pressing them firmly together.

3 Heat the oil in a deep-fat fryer or deep frying pan to about 180°C (350°F), or until a scrap of pastry dropped into the oil becomes crisp and golden, with a slightly blistered surface, in 15–20 seconds. If the oil starts to smoke, it is too hot. Add the cannoli, a couple at a time, and deep-fry until golden and crisp. Remove with tongs and drain on paper towels. As soon as the tubes are cool enough to handle, slide them out and leave the pastries on a rack to cool.

4 To make the filling, mash ricotta with a fork. Mix in the sugar and vanilla extract, then mix in the lemon zest, candied peel, glacé cherries and chocolate. Fill the pastries, either with a piping bag or a spoon. Arrange on a plate and dust with icing sugar. The cannoli should be eaten soon after they are filled.

APPLE TART

1 quantity sweet pastry (see page 149)

PASTRY CREAM

3 egg yolks

60 g (2½ oz/¼ cup) caster (superfine) sugar

15 g (½ oz) cornflour (cornstarch)

10 g (¼ oz) plain (all-purpose) flour

250 ml (9 fl oz/1 cup) milk

1 vanilla pod

15 g (½ oz) butter

4 dessert apples

80 g (3 oz) apricot jam

1   **To make the pastry cream,** whisk together the egg yolks and half the sugar until pale and creamy. Sift in cornflour and flour and mix well. Put the milk, remaining sugar and vanilla pod in a saucepan. Bring just to the boil, then strain over the egg yolk mixture, stirring continuously. Pour back into a clean saucepan and bring to the boil, stirring constantly. The mixture will be lumpy at first, but will become smooth as you are stirring. Boil for 2 minutes, then stir in the butter and leave to cool. Transfer to a clean bowl, lay plastic wrap on the surface to prevent a skin forming. Refrigerate and use within 2 days.

2   **Preheat the oven to** 180°C (350°F/Gas 4). Roll out the pastry to line a 23 cm (9 inch) round loose-based fluted tart tin. Chill in the fridge for 20 minutes.

3   **Line the pastry shell** with a crumpled piece of baking paper and baking beads (use dried beans or rice if you don't have beads). Blind bake the pastry for 10 minutes, remove the paper and beads and bake for a further 3–5 minutes, or until the pastry is just cooked but still very pale.

4   **Fill the pastry** with the pastry cream (also known as crème pâtissière). Peel and core the apples, cut them in half and then into thin slices. Arrange over the top of the tart and bake for 25–30 minutes or until the apples are golden and the pastry is cooked. Leave to cool completely, then melt the apricot jam with 1 tablespoon water, sieve out any lumps and brush over the apples to make them shine.

CHERRY CLAFOUTIS

SERVES 6–8

500 g (1 lb 2 oz) fresh cherries (see Note)

90 g (3 oz/¾ cup) plain (all-purpose) flour

2 eggs, lightly beaten

90 g (3 oz/⅓ cup) caster (superfine) sugar

250 ml (9 fl oz/1 cup) milk

60 ml (2 fl oz/¼ cup) thick (double/ heavy) cream

60 g (2 oz) unsalted butter, melted

icing (confectioners') sugar, for dusting

1 **Preheat the oven** to 180°C (350°F/Gas 4). Lightly grease a 1.5 litre (51 fl oz/6 cup) ovenproof dish with melted butter.

2 **Pit the cherries** and spread into the dish in a single layer.

3 **Sift the flour into a bowl,** add the eggs and whisk until smooth. Add the sugar, milk, cream and butter, whisking until just combined. Do not overbeat.

4 **Pour the batter** over the cherries and bake for 30–40 minutes, or until a skewer comes out clean when inserted into the centre. Dust generously with icing sugar before serving. Serve warm, straight from the oven.

Note: You can use a 720 g (1 lb 9 oz) jar of cherries if fresh ones aren't available. Make sure you drain it thoroughly before using the cherries.

PANNA COTTA

SERVES 4

500 ml (17 fl oz/2 cups) thick (double/heavy) cream

4 tablespoons caster (superfine) sugar

natural vanilla extract

3 sheets or 1¼ teaspoons gelatine

250 g (9 oz) fresh berries

1 **Put the cream and sugar in a saucepan** and stir over gentle heat until the sugar has dissolved.

2 **Bring to the boil,** then simmer for 3 minutes, adding a few drops of vanilla extract to taste.

3 **If using the gelatine sheets,** soak in cold water until they are floppy, then squeeze out any excess water. Stir the sheets into the hot cream until they are completely dissolved. If you are using powdered gelatine, sprinkle it onto the hot cream in an even layer and leave it to sponge for a minute, then stir it into the cream until dissolved.

4 **Pour the cream mixture** into four 125 ml (4 fl oz/½ cup) dariole moulds, cover each with a piece of plastic wrap and refrigerate until set.

5 **Unmould the panna cotta** by wrapping the moulds in a cloth dipped in hot water and tipping them gently onto individual plates. Serve with the fresh berries.

FIGS WITH ROSEWATER, ALMONDS AND HONEY

SERVES 6

12 fresh purple-skinned figs

50 g (2 oz/⅓ cup) blanched almonds, lightly toasted

3–4 teaspoons rosewater

1–2 tablespoons honey

1 **Wash the figs gently** and pat them dry with paper towel. Starting from the stem end, cut each fig into quarters, almost to the base, then gently open out and put on a serving platter. Cover and chill in the refrigerator for 1 hour, or until needed.

2 **Roughly chop** the toasted almonds and set aside.

3 **Carefully drizzle** about ¼ teaspoon of the rosewater onto the exposed centres of each of the figs, and sprinkle the chopped almonds over the top. Drizzle a little honey over the nuts. Serve immediately.

TARTE TATIN

SERVES 8

1.5 kg (3 lb 5 oz) dessert apples

70 g (2 oz) unsalted butter

170 g (6 oz/¾ cup) caster (superfine) sugar

TART PASTRY

220 g g (8 oz/1¾ cups) plain (all-purpose) flour

a pinch of salt

150 g (5½ oz) unsalted butter, chilled and diced

1 egg yolk

CRÈME CHANTILLY

185 ml (6 fl oz/¾ cup) thick (double/ heavy) cream

1 teaspoon icing (confectioners') sugar

½ teaspoon natural vanilla extract

1 Peel, core and cut the apples into quarters. Put the butter and sugar in a deep 25 cm (10 inch) frying pan with an ovenproof handle. Heat until the butter and sugar have melted together. Arrange the apples tightly, one by one, in the frying pan, making sure there are no gaps. Remember that you will be turning the tart out the other way up, so arrange the apple pieces so that they are neat underneath.

2 Cook over low heat for 35–40 minutes, or until the apple is soft, the caramel lightly browned and any excess liquid has evaporated. Baste the apple with a pastry brush every so often, so that the top is caramelized as well.

To make the pastry, sift the flour and salt into a large bowl, add the butter and rub in with your fingertips until the mixture resembles breadcrumbs. Add the egg yolk and a little cold water and mix with the blade of a knife until the dough just starts to come together. Shape into a ball. Wrap in plastic wrap and refrigerate for at least 30 minutes. Then, on a lightly floured surface, roll out the pastry into a circle slightly larger than the frying pan and about 3 mm (⅛ inch) thick. Preheat the oven to 190°C (375°F/Gas 5). Lay the pastry over the apple. Press down around the edge to enclose it completely. Roughly trim the edge of the pastry and then fold the edge back on itself to give a neat finish.

3 Bake for 25–30 minutes, or until the pastry is golden and cooked. Remove from the oven and leave to rest for 5 minutes before turning out swiftly and firmly. (If any apple sticks to the pan, just push it back into the hole in the tart.)

4 To make the crème chantilly, put the cream, icing sugar and vanilla extract in a chilled bowl. Whisk until soft peaks form and then serve with the hot tarte tatin.

PEARS COOKED IN RED WINE

SERVES 4

4 firm, ripe pears, peeled and cored

80 ml (3 fl oz/⅓ cup) lemon juice

250 ml (9 fl oz/1 cup) dry red wine

2 cinnamon sticks

220 g (8 oz/1 cup) sugar

8 slices lemon

1 Rub the pears with the lemon juice. Put the red wine, cinnamon sticks, sugar, lemon slices and 250 ml (9 fl oz/1 cup) water in a saucepan over low heat and simmer gently until the sugar dissolves. Bring to the boil, then reduce the heat and simmer for about 15 minutes. Add the pears and simmer for a further 20 minutes, carefully turning occasionally to ensure even colouring. Leave the pears to soak in the syrup overnight, if possible.

2 Remove the pears and simmer the syrup over high heat for about 15 minutes, or until it thickens slightly.

3 Serve the pears whole, drizzled with the syrup.

INDEX

INDEX